nervous water

BOOKS BY STEVE RAYMOND

Kamloops: An Angler's Study of the Kamloops Trout

The Year of the Angler

The Year of the Trout

Backcasts: A History of the Washington Fly Fishing Club
1939–1989

Steelhead Country

The Estuary Flyfisher

Rivers of the Heart

Blue Upright

nervous water

VARIATIONS ON A THEME OF FLY FISHING

STEVE RAYMOND

Illustrations by August C. Kristoferson

THE LYONS PRESS
Guilford, Connecticut
An imprint of The Globe Pequot Press

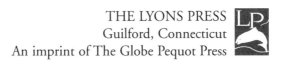

To buy books in quantity for corporate use
or incentives, call **(800) 962–0973, ext. 4551,**
or e-mail **premiums@GlobePequot.com.**

The Lyons Press is an imprint of The Globe Pequot Press.

10 9 8 7 6 5 4 3 2 1

Printed in the United States of America

Designed by Maggie Peterson

ISBN-10: 1-59228-884-7
ISBN-13: 978-1-59228-884-7

Library of Congress Cataloging-in-Publication Data is available on file.

FOR DAVE DRAHEIM

(even if he does sometimes fish with gaudy streamer patterns)

CONTENTS

PREFACE

Nervous water: Sometimes it's nothing more than a fleeting crease or wrinkle on the surface of a lake or stream, or a small patch of salt water that looks almost as if it's shivering. But wise anglers know such subtle surface movements are nearly always signs of fish stirring down below.

The sport of fly fishing is like that. It has a reputation for being a tranquil, contemplative sport—"a calm, quiet, innocent recreation," in Izaak Walton's words—but something is nearly always going on down below: constant currents of new thought and theory, a relentless drive to develop new technologies, an ongoing muted chorus of debate. Just as nervous water betrays the presence of moving fish, subtle ripples and distortions in the usually smooth outward fabric of fly fishing are often evidence of important things happening down below.

I have been involved in fly fishing as both participant and observer for more than half a century. During that time there have been many changes in the sport: a huge increase in its popularity, amazing progress in its technology, an unprecedented growth of its literature and a dramatic evolution in anglers' attitudes. Nobody could live through such a period without forming some pointed conclusions about whether all these changes have been healthy for the sport, and I have probably formed more than my share.

Many of these observations have been voiced in presentations to various gatherings of fly fishers over the years. Others were expressed in articles or essays published in numerous magazines, including *The*

Flyfisher, Sports Illustrated, FlyFishing (later *Western FlyFishing*), and *Fly Fisherman*. These articles and essays have considered many topics, some important (such as the very definition of fly fishing itself), and some trivial (such as how, or even whether, to dress for fishing).

Now, for the first time, many of these works have been collected in a single book—thirty-four variations on a theme of fly fishing. Together they form a selective, opinionated chronicle of trends, developments and changes in fly fishing from the 1960s to the present, plus a look back at some pioneers of the sport—and the fish that make it all possible.

Most of these pieces have been updated, expanded or otherwise revised or edited for publication in this book; several others appear here for the first time. With two exceptions, all are true or based on fact. The exceptions use fiction as a device to make a point more effectively; they should be obvious to readers, but just in case they aren't, they are identified in the "Author's Notes" section at the back of the book. That section also lists the forum or publication where each work first appeared.

Most of these pieces were written just for fun and are not intended to be taken very seriously, but some have a serious underlying message—which brings us back to the "nervous water" theme: Anglers should always study surface clues to understand what's happening down below. That's also true for some of the essays in this book, and it's another reason why *Nervous Water* seemed an apt title.

I enjoyed writing these pieces. I hope you will enjoy reading them.

—*Steve Raymond*
Clinton, Washington

Part One

"A Calm, Quiet, Innocent Recreation"

Brown trout are fond of lying in shady spots. Rainbow trout, on the other hand, like to lie in bright sunshine. Trout fishermen are never fussy about where they lie. Listen for them in your neighborhood tackle shop.

—MILFORD "STANLEY" POLTROON (DAVE BASCOM),
HOW TO FISH GOOD, 1971

Some consider fly fishing a chance for "lifestyle" dressing, others wear only the drabbest, oldest clothes they can find.

—NICK LYONS, *A FLYFISHER'S WORLD,* 1996

By the Book

North American trout and salmon waters fairly bristle with fly rods these days, thanks largely to the ever-increasing number of fly-fishing schools sponsored by tackle manufacturers, angling clubs and sporting-goods shops. Such schools have brought expert casting instruction within range of almost everyone, which is quite a contrast with the way things used to be. There was a time, not so very long ago, when many would-be fly fishers learned casting the hard way—by teaching themselves.

I know, because I was one of them. My only help was a book about casting. It was filled with photos and diagrams that made the whole thing look easy, and it inspired me to go out and purchase a new fly rod, plus matching line and reel, and set out to learn to cast.

Not having any water conveniently at hand, and feeling the self-consciousness of a beginner, I chose an empty pasture as a place to start. It was a cold, snowy weekend in February when I first went out in the pasture. The hay had been cut in late summer, leaving a sharp stubble that was now frozen and sticking up through the snow, but I didn't consider the consequences this might have for my new fly line. I was too intent on learning.

Consulting diagrams in the book, which I had brought along for handy reference, I soon learned that fly casting is a two-handed proposition: One hand holds the rod while the other keeps tension on the line. This means both hands are engaged simultaneously doing very different things. It's a little like trying to pat yourself on the head with one hand while rubbing your tummy with the other.

Getting the hang of that was difficult enough, but the real problem was what to do with the book. With both hands occupied there was no convenient way to hold it, and the snow would ruin it if I put it on the ground. I tried clutching it between my knees or sticking it inside my belt, but both were uncomfortable. I finally discovered I could hold it precariously by sandwiching it between my ribs and the elbow of my casting arm, although my casting motion was somewhat inhibited as a result.

(Later I was interested to learn that a traditional British method of casting instruction calls for the student to place a book under his casting arm and hold it there by pressing it against his side. This is supposed to teach him to keep his elbow close to his side, which the British apparently consider good form, but I wonder if the tradition wasn't really started by someone who learned to cast the same way I did—from a book he literally couldn't put down.)

All that first day I flailed away in the pasture, pausing only to refer to the book or to pick away at the knots that formed in my line and quickly froze. The cold seeped through my shoes and soon my feet were numb, but I didn't mind—perhaps because I was preoccupied with the pain in my casting arm, where the sharp corners of the book were wearing away the skin of my biceps.

Progress was slow and by the time winter darkness fell in the afternoon it was all I could do to get out twenty-five feet of line, and then only about once in every three or four tries. But my initial feeling of discouragement went away just as soon as I was able to thaw out my feet in front of a woodstove.

Next morning I started out with renewed determination and results came more rapidly. By early afternoon I had made a long cast of forty-five feet and was hitting forty feet with fair consistency. The knots and tangles were less frequent and I no longer felt the need to consult the book so often. But then, just as I was starting to gain confidence, my casts started falling short again. No matter how hard I tried, forty feet suddenly seemed an impossible distance. Something obviously was wrong.

I stopped then to take a close look at my new fly line, and the cause of my difficulty was immediately apparent. Hours of beating on the frozen stubble had worn away the finish on the line, reducing it to a long length of fuzz. It was like trying to cast a forty-foot caterpillar. Fortunately, the line was a double taper, the kind you can switch around after one end has worn out and use the other. When I did that, forty-foot casts became possible again.

The book described many different casts—backhand casts, negative and positive curves, switch casts, change-of-direction casts and others. At the outset, I felt I had to learn them all in order to be a proficient fisherman. But after two days of struggling in the pasture, I decided that being able to deposit a fly on the water in front of me, with the line between the fly and my rod more or less straight, was enough to start with.

For about ten days after that first weekend I suffered a bad cold and a sore arm, but as soon as the ill effects wore off I resumed practicing, looking forward to the mid-April opening of trout season when I could test my new skill in earnest. Finally the big day came and I drove to a swampy lake that was reputed to hold some large brook trout.

Small flies were hovering over the surface of the lake and when I got out of the car several of them promptly settled on my hands and neck and bit me. Following the traditional fly fisherman's precept of "matching the hatch," I selected a size 16 Mosquito pattern and tied it to the end of my leader. Then I launched my cartop boat and began rowing slowly along the shoreline, watching for signs of a feeding fish.

After a while I saw the dorsal fin of a large trout gently cleave the calm surface, leaving an impressive ripple in its wake. Conveniently, it was only about forty feet away.

With mounting excitement, I got to my feet and began switching the rod back and forth, working out line. At what I thought was just the right moment, I let go and threw hard at the spot where the trout had risen. Loops of line flew in a great blur and I was vaguely aware that something had gone terribly wrong. I wasn't immediately sure what, however, because by then my eyes were tightly closed.

When I opened them again I could see the line on the water. It went straight out for about ten feet, then curved back on itself. I followed it with my eyes, back to the boat, up over the side, down onto the deck, twice around my shoe, then up my leg. At about knee level the line ended and the leader began. Tracing it with a finger, I followed the leader up the rest of my leg, past my belt, up to my chin, past my mouth—and into my left nostril.

Somewhere, inside my nose, was a size 16 dry fly.

Slowly, carefully, I put down the rod. Now I could feel the hackles of the tiny fly tickling the inside of my nostril, and I clenched my teeth and fought back a terrible urge to sneeze. Gingerly—very gingerly—I took hold of the leader, praying the hook hadn't caught inside my nose. Still gritting my teeth, I gave the leader a gentle tug. The fly popped out cleanly.

After that I sat down, shook for a while, and wiped my watering eyes. The trout was long gone, of course, and as I recall I couldn't get within forty feet of another all the rest of that day.

But on my next trip I caught a few trout, and the trip after that yielded a few more, and by the end of my first season as a fly caster I had reason to believe that no trout could feel safe if it came even within fifty feet of me. What's more, I was even beginning to feel reasonably safe myself.

Now, after many decades of practice and experience, I can cast just about as far as I want and even hold my own with all those folks who went to school. And right about this point you probably expect the moral of the story—something about how being a self-taught caster builds character, teaches humility and inspires greater appreciation for the sport.

Well, you're wrong. The moral is that if I had to do it all over again, I wouldn't. I'd go to one of those schools instead.

SHOP SCENTS

To an angler, the fragrances of the finest bakeries or delicatessens are no more tantalizing than those of a good fly-fishing shop. The delicious smoky scent of fly-rod varnish, the satisfying redolence of the beeswax and pine pitch used on fly-tying thread, and even the whiff of mothballs, are every bit as appealing to a fly fisher as the aroma of a delicate pastry or a wedge of fine cheese.

For me, these and other familiar shop scents rekindle many bright memories, going all the way back to the shop in the small Northwest city where I was born. My father often took me there and I looked forward to those visits almost as much as I looked forward to going fishing itself.

The shop was large and dark and drafty, but it always had a strong smell of new leather from the belts and hunting boots on display. Along one wall was a heavy glass case, trimmed in wood, with sliding doors that opened only on the side where the clerks stood. The case held all kinds of gleaming treasures: handsome fly reels, shining steel knives, compasses in leather cases and large compartmented wooden trays brimming over with colorful trout flies. I spent many pleasant moments with my face pressed up against the side of that glass case, admiring its contents, listening to the quiet fishing talk of the men who always seemed to be present in the store, and breathing the rich, pungent smell of new leather.

When I was eight years old we moved to Yorktown, Virginia, a historic village too small to have a tackle shop. But it didn't really need one because it had Tignor's Store instead.

Tignor's was locally famous for the astonishing quantity and variety of goods its owner had managed to cram into a small space. I liked it because it had the same leathery smell as the tackle shop back home, but there was something else, too—a sort of warm, musty smell that seemed to have been baked into the small building by years of Virginia sunshine.

Most of Tignor's stock was in cardboard boxes—boxes of every size and shape, stacked from floor to ceiling against all four walls so that all the windows were covered and the only illumination was from a naked lightbulb hanging on a long cord. When you went to Tignor's you didn't go to look at the merchandise; you asked for what you wanted and Tignor would begin sorting and opening boxes until he found it, which he almost always did.

I don't remember buying any fishing tackle there—although I have no doubt Tignor had some boxed away—but I do remember an urgent trip to Tignor's to buy a tube of model-airplane cement, which I needed to complete some project. Tignor searched through many boxes until he found a small one that had never been opened. He slit open the paper seal and revealed tubes of model-airplane cement still in the same neat rows in which the manufacturer had packed them. I paid for one and rushed home, where I discovered on the first squeeze that the tube was as hard as a rock. It probably had been in Tignor's store since before I was born.

That was another thing about Tignor's: Although he nearly always had what you wanted, you could never be certain it was fresh.

Later, after I returned to the Northwest and began tying flies, I became a frequent patron of Patrick's Fly Shop in Seattle. Established in 1946, for many years it was the only fly shop in the area and was a place where local fly fishers gathered frequently to exchange information and tall tales. It was worth going there for that reason alone, even if you weren't in need of tying materials.

Roy Patrick, the shop's proprietor, was an irascible Irishman who was a better conversationalist than he was businessman, and it was common for customers to have to wait until the end of a long-winded fishing discourse before Patrick would deign to take their money and sell them the materials they wanted. Like most patrons of his shop, I soon learned never to ask Patrick about the state of his health; that was always good for at least a fifteen-minute monologue.

But if there was some exotic or obscure material you needed, you could almost always be certain that Patrick would have it in stock. He kept an amazing variety of materials, tucked away in drawers or stored in large glass jars on shelves that extended all the way to the ceiling. His shop reeked with the odor of mothballs, which got even stronger when he opened one of those drawers or jars. I shudder to think of the mess that would have resulted, or how it would have smelled, if there had ever been an earthquake strong enough to topple those jars off the shelves.

I remained a loyal customer of Patrick's for many years—after all, there was no place else to go—but when I heard another fly shop had opened in the hills northeast of Vancouver, British Columbia, I quickly made plans to check it out. After following a convoluted route over potholed back roads, I found the place in a remodeled barn in a small clearing in the woods. It was an unlikely location for a store of any kind, but what I found inside was even more surprising: a whole shelf of fine English-made fly reels at bargain prices, a sheaf of new fly rods in the corner, a barrelful of imported Indian gamecock necks for fly tying, and a huge assortment of other feathers, furs and synthetic materials. Again, the atmosphere was thick with the scent of anti-moth crystals, an odor that repels many people but always makes a fly tyer feel at home.

Finding that shop was like discovering a secret trout-filled beaver pond, the kind of place you keep to yourself or share with only a few trusted friends.

One doesn't ordinarily associate the aroma of tea with tackle shops, but the scent of Earl Grey or Orange Spice always reminds me of one of the most unusual shops I ever saw, a little place called the Red Spinner in the settlement of Hatepe on the eastern shore of New Zealand's Lake Taupo. Hardly larger than a small travel trailer, the shop contained only a bare counter, a single shelf with a few fly reels on display, and a pair of wooden chests with shallow drawers. The usual tackle-shop scents were absent; this place smelled only of tea.

The proprietor, whose name I later learned was Bruno Kemball, was standing behind the empty counter when I entered. I had been searching for a locally manufactured knockoff version of a famous English fly reel, and after glancing at the meager stock I asked Kemball without much hope if he had one. He glared at me, drew himself up to full height and spoke in a frosty English accent: "Young man, I learned long ago never to compromise on English quality. I advise you to do the same. I carry only genuine English-made reels."

Properly chastised, I then asked if he might recommend some flies for the Tongariro River, where I was bound. Without another word he went quickly to one of the wooden chests, selected a drawer and opened it. Inside were some of the most beautiful trout flies I had ever seen, arranged in meticulous order on a layer of velvet. "You'll need two of these," he said, using a pair of tweezers to pick up a pair of the flies and place them carefully in a small cellophane envelope as if they were rare postage stamps. He went to another drawer and repeated the process, continuing until at last he handed me half a dozen cellophane envelopes, each containing two flies. "For the Tongariro," he said.

I paid him, mumbled thanks, and went outside, feeling as if I had just left No. 10 Downing Street.

A day or two later, while I was fishing on the Tongariro, I mentioned the experience to another angler. "Let me tell you about the first time I went to the Red Spinner," he said. "Old Bruno was busy with another customer, so I thought I'd save time and help myself. I went over to the chest, opened a drawer and was just reaching in for a fly when Bruno caught me across the wrist with a karate chop. 'I'll thank you to keep your bloomin' 'ands off my flies!' he says. 'Next time use the bloody tweezers; that's what they're for!'"

I've sampled the atmosphere of many other tackle shops, including some very famous ones—Dan Bailey's and Bud Lilly's in Montana, Kaufmann's Streamborn in Seattle and dozens of others. Each was filled with "all the delicious paraphernalia that drives us nuts," as Nick Lyons once put it so eloquently. Each also had its own personality, its own atmosphere, its own peculiar scent, and I've never been in one I didn't like.

But the most famous shops are usually also the largest, and fishing has become a very big business in recent years. As a result, the shops, the salesmen and the sport itself have all become a little less personal, and some of the charm has gone out of all of them.

Yet the shops still smell pretty much the same as they always have, and whenever I enter one and recognize those old familiar scents I still feel something of the excitement of a small boy with his face pressed up against a glass case full of gleaming treasures, breathing the rich scent of new leather and listening to the fishing talk that never seems to change.

THE FINE ART OF
FLYFINAGLING

Library shelves groan under the weight of the accumulated angling literature of the centuries. By far the largest share of the output has been devoted to fly fishing and has dealt with every conceivable aspect and angle of the sport—except one. A certain highly developed and widely practiced part of the sport has not only been largely ignored by the great angling writers of the ages but continues to go unnoticed until this day.

It's time this deplorable state of affairs was remedied, time this noble art should be accorded its rightful place of honor alongside streamcraft, entomology, fly tying and the other skills of fly fishing. Moreover, guidance should be made available to those who aspire to become the experts of tomorrow.

We speak, of course, of the practice generally referred to by the cognoscenti as the Fine Art of Flyfinagling.

It's probably true that every fly fisher has at one time or another been a flyfinagler, either consciously or unconsciously. However, as in so many other things, we tend to regard this aspect of the sport as a part of the whole rather than a separate skill in itself. Therefore, for the edification of those not familiar with flyfinagling, let me explain the basic rudiments of the art.

Let us say you are knee-deep in your favorite dry-fly water and evening is coming on fast. A hatch of some kind is getting under way. Soon the air is filled with mayflies. These are the creatures most angling authors refer to with adjectives such as *dainty*, *graceful*, *gossamer* and other nonmasculine terms. Some even go so far as to say the flies "floated past like a tiny fleet of painted sailboats," et cetera.

Reminding yourself that you are a fly fisher, you resist the impulse to swat the nasty bugs and reach out carefully to capture one of the creatures in your hand, trying very hard not to mangle it. You hold it up for close inspection and, if you are an angling author, you say something like, "Aha! *Ephemera simulans*, no doubt about it." If not, you likely say something like, "Hmmm, this little critter is gray, that's for sure." You reach in your fly box and search for something that remotely resembles the natural, which by now is nothing but a wipe along your index finger.

Fortunately you find something sufficiently imitative to fool a couple of trout. While you play your fish you are suddenly aware that another angler has splashed his way within a dozen paces. Self-consciously, you lift your latest conquest from the water and—again reminding yourself that you are a fly fisher and, therefore, a conservationist—you return it to the stream.

The other angler looks on with swollen eyes.

"M'Gawd," he says. "What'd you take 'im on?"

"Oh, just a little pattern I tied myself," you say modestly. You show him the fly.

"Geez," he says, "I don't have anything that looks like that. And I haven't taken a fish all day."

Filled with pity for this poor fellow whose intelligence has failed him to the point that he has no size 12 Gray Parachute Woollies in his pocket, you generously give him a couple.

"Wow, thanks," he says, and scrambles for the bank.

Feeling you have done your good deed for the day, you resume fishing. On your next cast a twenty-inch trout seizes the fly, snaps the leader and swims off with your size 12 Gray Parachute Woollie in its mouth. Looking for another in your fly box, you discover, naturally, that you have just given away your last two.

Later you meet the other angler on the bank, staggering under a bulging creel. With tears of sincerity in his eyes, he thanks you again for your generosity.

Don't look now, but you have just been finagled.

Now that you know what this aspect of the sport is all about, let us look at some of the historical precedents. Flyfinagling, you see, is nothing new.

In an obscure, seldom-published version of Dame Juliana Berners' seminal work, *The Treatyse on Fysshynge with an Angle*, we find this reference to flyfinagling:

> Bewaare t' mon who cometh upon ye wyth oystrytched hond
> on the Ryvere and prayses the flyese wyth whcyh yr fish. Lykely
> it is that hy is foul bynt and wyshes onlye to depryve ye of your
> prycious flyese whyle he flattyrs ye wyth hys glyb tongue.
>
> Byt on t' othyr hond, don't ye be afrayd to try it yoursylf.

Likewise, Venator, whose angling instruction by Piscator was chronicled by Izaak Walton, often was heard to complain that somehow or other he always ended up with an empty fly box after a day with Piscator on the stream.

Legend has it that the great orator Daniel Webster once took a mighty, forty-pound trout from the Carmans River on Long Island.

While angling history makes little note of any other accomplishments by Webster, there can be no doubt that he was one of history's greatest flyfinaglers. The fact is that the great trout was taken by Webster on a fly he finagled from another angler he encountered on the stream. With his great oratorical skill, it was a simple task for Webster to use a few well-chosen words to reduce the other angler to the point of tears and induce him to hand over his entire assortment of flies.

The fine art of flyfinagling also is responsible for some of the great discoveries of fly fishing. Though it is not widely known, G. E .M. Skues used to bum his flies from the great Frederic Halford. Finally, in exasperation, Halford told Skues to go jump in the Itchen and learn to tie his own flies.

Skues tried, but he had a great deal of difficulty getting his dry flies to float properly. The sunken flies still caught fish, however, and Skues claimed for himself the invention of nymph fishing.

It also is generally not known that the reason Halford stopped giving flies to Skues was that Halford finagled all of his from his friend, George Selwyn Marryat, who was running low.

Today flyfinagling is an art practiced by many who are more skilled in it than in the actual process of angling itself. It is especially for these anglers, whose skill is insufficient to warrant recognition for other feats, that I believe awards for finagling should be established.

But regardless of whether any form of recognition is established, a silent legion of anglers bent on finagling will continue to haunt our trout streams and lakes.

My advice is to keep your fly box closed.

JUNKYARD RIVERS

It was a fine day for fishing and the river seemed in perfect shape. The current carried my fly down through a long, deep, promising drift. No trout took hold, but as I followed the progress of the fly I noticed a metallic glint under the water.

Wading downstream to investigate, I could see the outline of a large object on the bottom, mostly hidden by a layer of fine gravel the river had swept over it. I kicked at it with my waders until enough gravel had fallen away to reveal what it was.

Would you believe a penny gumball machine?

That wasn't all. In a short stretch of river I found four others. Each had its coin box pried open. A thief had collected them somewhere, rifled their coin boxes, then dumped them off an upstream bridge. He'd also taken all the gum out of them.

The gumball machines were in the Cedar River, southeast of Seattle. The Cedar was a fairly pristine stream in those days, but being close to an urban area it inevitably attracted its share of society's debris. In fact, it's a rare river anywhere nowadays that doesn't contain at least a few rusting automobile hulks, bedsprings, scads of beer and soda-pop cans and plenty of other miscellaneous trash. Some is dumped on purpose and some by accident, and sometimes rivers scoop up a lot of it on their own when they overflow their banks.

One result is that if you fish rivers a lot, you come across some pretty odd things.

A friend once noticed a shiny object on the bottom of a river he was fishing. Thinking it was a marble, he stooped to pick it up. It turned out to be a glass eye.

Another angling friend reported finding a trombone in a river.

Most of the odd things I've found have been in the North Fork of the Stillaguamish. I own a small fishing cabin on the North Fork and fish it often.

One day I was wading the river near my cabin when I noticed a round green object on the bottom. It was a pool ball—the No. 6 ball, to be exact. Within a short time I found ten other balls from the same set, plus the cue ball.

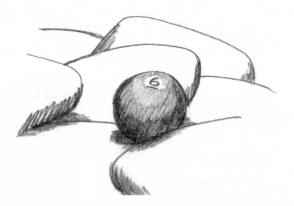

I don't know what happened to the four balls missing from the set; presumably, being round, they washed downstream, perhaps as far as Puget Sound. If I pick up a newspaper someday and read that a fisherman has landed a big chinook salmon with a 13 ball in its stomach, I won't be surprised.

It's fun to speculate how a nearly complete set of pool balls ended up in the river. Even more intriguing is to speculate about what happened to the table. As far as I know, nobody has reported seeing any pool tables floating down the North Fork.

Some years ago the North Fork acquired a manure spreader. It probably was dumped in the river by a farmer or swept up in a flood. Eventually it became lodged in the Deer Creek Riffle, one of the most popular fishing spots on the river.

Within a season or two anglers discovered that the best place to fish the Deer Creek Riffle was from the middle of the manure spreader. If you waded out and stood right in the center of the rusting frame, then cast downstream, your chances of hooking a steelhead were good. The manure spreader became an important local angling landmark.

Then the river flooded, bringing down huge amounts of silt and gravel. The manure spreader now lies buried under many layers of flood debris.

Perhaps that was the same flood that washed down the carousel horse I found in the river. The horse now sits next to a trail near my cabin, its origin a complete mystery.

Years ago, one of my riverside neighbors set up a golf tee on the bank and started using the North Fork as a driving range. His son-in-law, who worked at a commercial driving range, kept him well supplied with balls. His best drives carried over the river and deep into the woods on the other side. Steelhead and salmon dodged his hooks and slices.

Occasionally fishermen ended up dodging, too. I remember once I was returning from a trip downriver, walking behind a screen of alders across the river from my neighbor's cabin. Suddenly golf balls began ripping through the foliage, dropping all around me. There were a couple of near misses, but fortunately no hits.

But getting bombarded by golf balls was a minor tribulation compared with what happened on the North Fork on October 19,

1959, the day the river acquired what undoubtedly ranks as its most spectacular bit of debris: A Boeing 707 on a test flight clipped the tops off several big firs near my cabin and crash-landed right in the middle of the North Fork's Elbow Hole, killing the crew. Fortunately, no fishermen were in its way.

Salvage crews removed the bulk of the airliner from the river, but until just a few years ago bits and pieces of wreckage could still be found on the gravel bars and in the woods across the river from my cabin. A series of floods finally buried what remained.

Which is just as well. It's bad enough having to cast from the middle of a manure spreader, or being forced to tease up a steelhead from the submerged skeleton of a 1968 Oldsmobile. But trying to catch fish from the tourist-class section of a Boeing 707—that's a bit too much.

DRESSING FOR SUCCESS

The other day I was interviewed by a fashion reporter—a fashion reporter!—who wanted to know what I thought about the latest in fly-fishing couture.

She looked her part. Her hair was absolutely perfect, like on one of those television shampoo commercials. She was dressed stylishly in expensive clothes that fit her flawlessly. My hair—what there is of it—stuck out at odd angles, and I was wearing rumpled polyester and a tie with a salad-dressing spot on it. I wondered if someone had referred her to me as a joke.

But I tried to answer her questions seriously and she wrote down my answers as if she was taking them seriously: Yes, fly-fishing fashions seem to have become a big deal for some people. Yes, it's a lot like skiing—you are what you wear, or at least some people think you are. Yes, you see a lot of people who look like they just stepped out of an Orvis or L.L. Bean catalog; they even have the same silly grins as the catalog models. No, trout don't seem to care much how you're dressed.

Thinking about it afterward, I realized that last answer was a bit presumptuous since I didn't really know how trout felt about the matter. Trout are such honest and uncompromising creatures—one of the things I like about them—that I supposed they couldn't care less how anglers dress. But I didn't really know; perhaps they *do* care.

I've always dressed pretty much the same when fishing—war-surplus scrounge (don't ask which war). Maybe if I tried dressing like an Orvis model I'd catch more trout.

Or maybe I wouldn't.

I decided to research the question. I began by trying to think of incidents in my angling experience when dress might have affected success. I could remember only two.

One was the time I joined a picket fence of anglers along the edge of a weed bed on a mountain lake in the soft light of an early summer evening, waiting for the start of the caddis hatch. Some of the anglers were in float tubes, others—including me—in small boats. I was wearing my usual fishing garb—a well-stained hat that had lost its shape several seasons back, its only distinguishing feature a Confederate officer's insignia my wife had sewn on it as a joke, along with a faded shirt, baggy jeans and an oversized jacket, one of those kind with pockets on top of pockets, all of them stuffed full of junk. I suppose from a distance you might have thought I was a bag lady.

But I wasn't thinking about my clothes. After a slow start the caddis hatch was getting into full swing, with big, succulent bugs skittering over the surface and occasional fish lurching up to gulp them. Soon I was busy casting to rises, hooking fish, playing them, releasing them. I hardly noticed that nobody else seemed to be doing much business; all I knew was that for once I had a hot hand and I was having a ball. I paid no attention to the murmured comments I could hear from other anglers up and down the line.

Then my friend Dave Draheim came up in his boat, pushing it forward with the oars. He was laughing so hard I thought he was going to choke.

"What's so funny?" I asked.

He gestured down the line at two very well-dressed fishermen in a driftboat next to another well-attired angler in a float tube. "Those guys were watching you play a fish when I went by," he said. "You know what one of them said? He said: 'Maybe that's what it takes: Dress like a bum and catch all the fish!'"

My first reaction was to feel mildly insulted. Bum indeed! But then it occurred to me that maybe the guy was actually on to something: He was certainly well dressed, but he wasn't catching any fish.

The other incident I remembered was a time I watched two anglers launch a bright, shiny new fiberglass canoe, climb in and shove off from the shore of Dry Falls Lake. Both men were dressed in the latest fashionable fishing togs, as bright and shiny as their new canoe, still bearing creases from mail-order shipment. I mean, these guys were Tarponweared, Orvised, L.L. Beaned and Eddie Bauered from head to foot.

I watched them paddle out a couple of hundred yards to a spot that apparently appealed to their unpracticed fishing eyes, then stop. One got rather unsteadily to his feet, unlimbered a new graphite rod and started casting. Then the other got up and also made a cast. Then the canoe rolled over.

Fortunately there were a lot of other fishermen in the vicinity and several went quickly to the rescue, plucking the two sputtering anglers out of the lake and even retrieving most of their brand-new gear. The hapless pair paddled slowly back to shore, their bright, shiny canoe now half full of water and their new clothes all water-logged and shapeless. Embarrassed for them, I averted my eyes, as did almost everyone else in the neighborhood. Nobody laughed, either, which just goes to show that fly fishers in general are kind, consider-ate folks.

So here was a pair of anglers dressed to the gills (if you'll pardon the expression) in fishing's finest fashions, and not only did they not catch any trout, but they almost ended up joining them. Admittedly, they hardly had time to do any fishing before their sudden immersion, but hey, this is research, and you cling to any factoid you can.

Of course these two incidents are hardly enough to form any definitive conclusions about whether trout prefer to be caught by well-dressed anglers or those who look like bums, but maybe some enterprising graduate student will carry the research to a conclusion. "Comparative Angling Success Rates Among Statistically Similar Groups of Fashionable and Unfashionable Fly Fishers" certainly would make a catchy thesis title.

Personally, I've always thought the primary considerations in dressing for fishing were comfort, protection against the elements and avoiding bright colors to keep from frightening trout. Fashion always has been furthest from my thoughts, doubtless evident to anyone who has ever seen me fishing. Nevertheless, as I told the fash-ion reporter, it's obvious that making a fashion statement is a high priority for lots of people these days, and they seem willing to spend lots of money to do it.

Spending money isn't always necessary, though. The most profound fly-fishing fashion statement I've ever seen didn't cost the angler a cent.

The occasion was a late Indian-summer day on Oregon's De-schutes River. Frank Amato and I were headed upstream in Frank's jet boat when we rounded a bend and I noticed another fisherman on the far side of the river, wading in the shallows and casting a fly so intently he didn't even look up as we passed.

Then I did a double take and looked again.

The fisherman was wearing Polaroid glasses, but that was all. Otherwise he was buck naked.

Top that for a fashion statement.

I told Frank I thought the guy might be trying to start a trend. He probably had a FISH NAKED bumper sticker on his car.

I didn't mention this incident during the interview with the fashion reporter. I was afraid that if she wrote about it, the trend might catch on.

On second thought, maybe I should have told her. If fishing naked becomes popular, we could all save money on clothes. Waders, too.

But then I'd have to lose weight, and I'd rather spend the money.

BEAR WITH ME

Take two or more anglers, open a couple of beers, and odds are you'll soon start hearing bear stories. That's because most veteran fly fishers have at least one good bear story they are always willing and anxious to tell, which isn't surprising considering bears and anglers are often found in the same places—along trout streams and salmon rivers.

I've had my own share of run-ins with bears. One of my portable food-and-beverage coolers has a large, triangular-shaped dent in the lid, a tooth mark left by a hungry bear that tried to carry off the cooler one night while I was camped at a mountain lake. Ordinarily I would never leave a cooler outside in bear country, but I'd been fishing that lake for thirty years without ever having seen a bear in the vicinity, and since that night I haven't seen another.

Then there was the dark night at a remote fishing camp when I was halfway up the trail to the outdoor privy when I suddenly became aware of a darkness more than night directly in my front. Switching on my flashlight, I found the path blocked by a bear that looked ten feet tall, and we were close enough to shake hands. We didn't, though; within a split second we each did an about-face and started running as fast we could in opposite directions.

Another time I was backing my Jeep down to the shore of a lake so I could launch my cartop boat and go fishing. Looking in the rearview mirror to make sure I wasn't getting too close to the lake's edge, I was more than a little surprised to see a bear looking back at me. This was a well-behaved bear, though; it moved politely out of the way so I could finish backing down, then kept a respectful distance while I launched my boat and went fishing.

It seems a lot of my bear experiences have been in British Columbia, which makes sense because I fish there often and that huge province has more bears than just about anyplace except Alaska.

One night Errol Champion and I were camped at BC's Roche Lake when we heard a commotion outside. Errol had just purchased a new strobe-light attachment for his camera and was anxious to try it out, so he grabbed the camera and I grabbed a flashlight and we dashed outside into the darkness and rain.

The flashlight disclosed a bear with its snout buried in a garbage can not far from our camp. Frightened by the light, the bear backed out of the garbage can and started running. Errol ran after it, fumbling with his camera, and I followed, shining the flashlight so Errol could see where he was going.

The bear dashed down a dirt road into a nearby meadow with the pair of us in hot pursuit. Once in the meadow's tall grass, the bear apparently felt safe and stopped to turn and look at the odd creatures following it. Errol and I also halted and I held the light while he focused the camera and clicked the shutter. The new strobe illuminated the meadow with a nuclear burst of light that left us both momentarily blinded.

That was when I heard a loud *grrrffff* behind me. Wheeling around, I aimed the flashlight in the direction of the sound. Through the sunspots of light still dancing in front of my eyes, I vaguely discerned the shape of another large bear not twenty-five feet away. It was almost as if the two bears had planned a perfect ambush, the first luring us down the road to the meadow while the second came up from behind.

But the second bear apparently had nothing malicious in mind, for when I hit him (or her) with the flashlight beam, the creature merely grunted, turned away and ambled off into the woods.

I don't remember how Errol's strobe-lit bear photograph turned out, but I'll never forget the circumstances under which it was taken.

Still, all these are pretty much run-of-the-mill bear stories, the kind of encounter almost any bear-country angler is likely to have. This next one, however, is definitely out of the ordinary; in fact, I think it's unique.

It happened in the late 1960s when my wife, Joan, and I were fishing at the Circle W fishing camp on British Columbia's famous Hihium Lake. Pat Kirkpatrick, who then owned the Circle W, had warned us about a bear that had been causing trouble around the lake. The large female had a pair of cubs, which would have made her touchy under any circumstances, but to make matters worse somebody had taken a shot at her and wounded her in the shoulder. The wound was infected and flyblown and the bear was understandably in a dangerously foul mood—so much so, Pat said, that he had felt compelled to call the BC Fish and Wildlife Branch in Kamloops and ask them to send out a game warden to put the animal down. Meanwhile, he advised us to keep a careful eye out for the bear and her cubs.

We fished a couple of days without seeing any sign of bears. Then, on our third morning, the caretaker who made daily rounds of the Circle W's remote cabins steered his boat to our dock and came up to the cabin to ask if we needed anything. We invited him in for a cup of coffee and he settled himself in a chair, took a couple of sips of coffee, and asked if we'd heard the big commotion over at Duck Point the night before.

Duck Point, about a quarter of a mile away, was the site of another cabin. When we told the caretaker we hadn't heard any noise
from that direction, he leaned back in his chair and began telling us
an interesting tale.

It seemed the four fishermen who were staying in the Duck
Point cabin had returned the previous evening with a large catch of
trout. When they had finished cleaning their catch they had, for reasons known only to themselves, hoisted the trout into a tree and left
them hanging there overnight—something nobody in his right mind
would ever do in bear country.

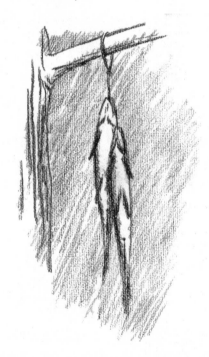

Needless to say, the scent of the freshly cleaned trout brought
the wounded bear and her two cubs out of the woods and they
made such a racket trying to reach the strung-up fish that the four
anglers were rudely awakened in the middle of the night. All four
rushed out onto the cabin porch, shouting and screaming and beat-

ing pots and pans with spoons. The noise frightened the bears, which disappeared back into the woods, whereupon the four anglers returned to their bunks.

No sooner had they fallen back asleep than the bears returned and woke them again. Once more the four fishermen tumbled out onto the porch, repeating their earlier cacophony, and once more the bears lumbered off into the woods. The unhappy anglers went back to bed.

And of course exactly the same thing happened a third time.

Finally, sometime around four o'clock in the morning, when the bears returned for the fourth time, one of the disgruntled anglers seized a .22-caliber rifle he had brought to shoot pack rats, opened a cabin window, and, without taking aim at anything in particular, squeezed off a shot or two. Frightened by the gunfire, the bears ran off again.

When daylight came, the four anglers—no doubt rubbing their sleep-deprived eyes—went outside to check on the fish. The fish were unmolested, but about a hundred feet from the cabin they found one of the bear cubs lying on its side, stone-cold dead.

They were still standing in a circle, looking down at the dead cub, when a boat pulled up at the Duck Point dock. It was the game warden Pat Kirkpatrick had summoned from Kamloops.

The warden came ashore, took one look, and pulled out his citation book. He wrote up the four anglers for hunting big game out of season without a license and ordered them to report to a magistrate in Kamloops the following Monday morning, where he said they could expect to receive stiff fines if not a jail sentence.

"That's quite a tale," I told the caretaker when he had finished. Then I had a thought: "What happened to the dead bear?"

"I've got him down in my boat."

"What are you going to do with him?"

"Take him over to my camp and bury him."

"Hmmm. Seems like a terrible waste of good fly-tying material."

"You want some? Grab your knife and come on down; you can have all you want."

So I took my knife and followed the caretaker down to his boat. The dead cub was large, probably in its second year, and appeared in very good condition, if you overlooked the fact that it was dead. It had a thick, luxuriant coat of long black hair, useful in several steelhead and Atlantic salmon fly patterns, so I cut a large square section out of its hide, thanked the caretaker, and took the patch of hair back to the cabin where I scraped off the fat, salted it down, and put it in the window to dry.

And that, as far as I was concerned, was the end of the business. It wasn't until the following week that I learned what happened later.

After leaving our cabin, the caretaker returned to his camp and was busy digging a hole to bury the dead cub when the game warden showed up again. The warden had spent several hours in an unsuccessful hunt for the wounded mother bear and now was on his way back to Kamloops.

"But first I need another look at that cub," he told the caretaker. "I never did take note of where the bullet went in."

The cub was lying on its side and the warden examined it carefully without finding anything. Then, with effort, he turned it over—and saw the huge square hole in its side.

"What in hell happened to this bear?" he demanded.

"Oh, some crazy fly tyer up the lake cut a piece out of its hide," the caretaker said.

Mumbling to himself, the game warden continued his inspection of the corpse, examining the bear carefully from stem to stern. But except for the large patch of missing hide, he didn't find a mark on it.

So when the four chastened anglers appeared in Kamloops court Monday morning, the magistrate was quick to dispose of the case. "It's the warden's own testimony that the only mark on the bear cub's body was where a fly tyer cut off a patch of hair," the magistrate said. "For all I know, the bear could have died of a heart attack. Case dismissed!"

And that, I think you will agree, is not your ordinary bear story.

Just in case you were wondering, I never did find a bullet hole in that patch of hair. Maybe the magistrate was right and the cub really did expire from a heart attack.

THE INTREPID
INSECT TRAPPER

Yes, I went through that phase, too—that period in many a fly fisher's life when looking at photos of mayflies and caddisflies in books just isn't good enough anymore. I wanted to be able to hold them right in my hand and study them closely, and the only way to do that was to go out and try to capture some of the real thing.

So I went to a scientific supply house and purchased an insect-collecting outfit: a whole case of sample bottles, a nifty little bug net, a two-quart plastic portable aquarium, even a microscope. I justified the expense of the latter on grounds that I could use it for reading fish scales (another phase I was going through at the time) as well as studying insects.

But I stopped short of buying any formalin or formaldehyde, or whatever stuff professional entomologists use to preserve their samples. That's because I couldn't stand the smell. Just a whiff was enough to remind me of visits to the county morgue when I was working as police reporter for a metropolitan newspaper, and I'd just as soon not be reminded of those occasions.

Instead, I went searching in books for another preservative formula. Eventually I found one that consisted of alcohol and one or two other ingredients; I forget now what they were. The formula seemed to work well enough at first, at least for everything but freshwater scuds. Put one of those little gray-green guys into the solution and the scud would turn bright orange before your eyes. Maybe that accounts for all the orange shrimp fly patterns you see in the fly shops. They might get you a fish in salt water, but in fresh water they stick out like brake lights on a sport-utility vehicle.

Like every other bug-hunting angler, I also soon discovered that collecting insects isn't as easy as you might think. Skimming them from the surface film takes patience, practice and care; I practiced and was careful, but my patience was in short supply. Nevertheless, after sloshing around several rivers chasing insects drifting rapidly downstream, and rowing frantically around several lakes trying to capture bugs that seemed as elusive as quicksilver, I managed to fill a goodly number of my sample bottles. It wasn't very long before I had a fairly impressive collection of mayflies, caddisflies and stoneflies in all stages of their life cycles, not to mention damselfly and dragonfly nymphs, chironomid pupae and adults, water boatmen and backswimmers, various other aquatic and terrestrial insects—and several bright orange scuds. I even started to practice pronouncing their Latin names until I could actually say things like *Limnephilus oslari* or *Phrygenea cinerea*. This came in very handy for one-upmanship in conversations with other fly fishers, especially when I realized that nobody else knew whether I was pronouncing the names correctly or not.

Sometimes I captured live mayfly nymphs or caddis pupae and put them in the portable aquarium, then sat back to watch them hatch, getting some remarkable close-up photos in the process. I used the microscope to try to identify adult mayflies and caddisflies—not just by genus (who wants to stop at that point?) but all the way down to individual species.

If you've ever tried to identify an insect species using a taxonomic key, then you know it's several times more complicated than filling out your income-tax return. I spent hours squinting through the slender tube of the microscope, contemplating vein patterns in mayfly wings and counting the number of spurs on the forelegs of caddisflies.

This was tedious work, but I persevered—mainly with caddisflies—until I was certain I had correctly identified several individual species. Then I read the results of work done by another angling entomologist whom I knew had more experience (and probably more patience) than I did. I also knew he'd been looking at exactly the same bugs I had, and I was shocked to see his findings were completely different from mine. I wasn't certain which of us was right, but I was pretty sure it wasn't me.

This troubled me until one day I was struck by a profound thought: What the hell difference did it make? I had learned enough from my insect-trapping efforts to tell one bug from another, and as long as I could identify insects by type and tie flies that were reasonable imitations, then what did it matter if I couldn't tell exactly what genus or species they represented?

I was also growing tired of lugging along bottles, net and aquarium whenever I went fishing. Furthermore, it occurred to me that this insect-chasing business was beginning to cut rather seriously into my fishing time. Clearly I had reached the point of diminishing returns.

It was just as well, because about that time I discovered the preservative formula I had been using was inexplicably evaporating from the sample bottles. Even when I screwed the bottle caps down tight and put several layers of tape around them, the stuff still somehow managed to escape, almost as if some sort of mysterious osmotic process was going on. As the preservative evaporated, large portions of the insect samples seemed to evaporate along with it, and when I went to check the bottles I found most of them empty except for little blobs of unidentifiable beige-colored matter in the bottoms. So much for my collecting efforts.

All that was many years ago. The spectacular close-up photos of all those hatching nymphs and pupae are now buried somewhere in a file cabinet. The portable aquarium is gathering dust on a shelf in my office. I don't know what happened to the insect net, but I think the kids took it when they discovered it was handy for dipping goldfish. I do know one of the kids absconded with the microscope.

The case full of sample bottles is still languishing somewhere on a shelf. I suppose if the bottles were cleaned and sterilized they might be useful for urine samples or something like that. I can't think what else to do with them.

Thus ended my career as an intrepid insect trapper. It was kind of fun while it lasted, and I'm certain I learned a lot, although I've probably forgotten most of it since. Well, maybe that's not quite true; I think the experience helped me gain what I'd like to think is a well-rounded fly-fishing education. In theory, at least, that should make me a better fisherman.

It also helped me become more tolerant of fellow anglers. Nowadays, when I see folks flailing around in a stream, waving a net in a frantic effort to catch a mayfly before it rises beyond reach, or desperately paddling a float tube across a lake in hopeless pursuit of a skittering caddisfly, I no longer automatically write them off as raving angling lunatics. I understand exactly what they're doing, and why.

I just hope their preservative formula works better than mine did.

ELKO INTERLUDE

Friday night in Elko, Nevada. After driving for hours on the interstate with little sign of traffic, it's a shock to pull off and find gridlock on Idaho Street, Elko's main thoroughfare. Here there is a solid line of Broncos, Blazers and pickup trucks, many wearing bumper stickers exhorting people to pray and/or protect their right to keep and bear arms. One particular favorite: Earth first! We'll mine other planets later.

The trucks are driven by workers who have come pouring out of the mines and off the ranches, mostly sinewy young men with hard sunburns and a week's growth of beard. They wear cowboy hats or baseball caps, heavy boots and gap-toothed grins, and they head for the casino bars to guzzle tasteless industrial beer and smoke cigarettes, letting the ashes fall and burn holes in the carpet. Later they will order a big steak and a huge platter of fries at one of Elko's Basque restaurants, then perhaps fulfill their remaining desires at one of the local "sporting houses."

Saturday morning: It's quiet now and the streets are empty. DO NOT DISTURB signs hang from the knobs of many motel-room doors while last night's celebrants sleep it off. The Hispanic maids who are supposed to clean the rooms throw up their hands and sigh, knowing it will be late afternoon before they can get inside to clean the last of them.

It's mid-October and the deer-hunting season is in full swing. The word around town is that if you're going to be outdoors for any reason, you'd better wear a flame-orange vest; otherwise some "hunter" who's spent the day getting hammered on cheap whiskey is likely to decide that, since you're moving, you must be a deer.

This is no joke. There are signs along the main routes asking people to report anyone seen shooting from the roadway, and rumor has it that an average of two people are shot around here every week. If you're an outdoorsman, your chances of being one of them are probably better than your chances of winning in one of the local casinos.

Of course, you can elect to defend yourself if you want to; here even the drugstores sell guns.

At a local sport shop I ask about the fishing, although it seems odd to be talking about fishing in a country as dry as this. The shop owner, a pudgy, bearded fellow with a high-pitched giggle, suggests the South Fork of the Humboldt River where it enters a nearby reservoir. There, he says, big browns are just beginning their fall spawning run. He sketches a map for me, and in return I buy some flies I don't really need. His cluttered shop looks like the room of a teenage boy who has defied his mother's orders to clean it up, but he seems to know where everything is amid the clutter.

Next we head for the local Kmart to buy a couple of ninety-nine-cent flame-orange vests.

Saturday night: The town has come alive again. In the bar at the Stockmen's Hotel & Casino, a young man wearing a pink shirt and white cowboy hat announces he has just married a girl wearing a tight fire-engine-red dress and dangling gold earrings. People gather around to offer congratulations and the new groom introduces his bride simply as "my wife," as if he can't remember—or perhaps doesn't know—her name.

Sunday morning: Joan and Randy and I drive to the South Fork of the Humboldt and park near a bridge half a mile upstream from the point where the river enters the reservoir. The hills are alive with the sound of gunfire.

Joan stays behind while Randy and I start downstream, me toting a fly rod and Randy a book. The South Fork is a small stream, very low at this season, barely six inches deep in most places. It meanders through a succession of shallow, nearly stagnant pools linked by brief stretches of weak current that scarcely qualify for the term *riffle*. At first we see dense clouds of fry but no sign of larger trout, but as we near the reservoir the pools begin to deepen a little and then Randy spies a trout of twelve or fourteen inches. Moments later I see another, this one larger, about two and a half pounds by my best guess. But even though I try to approach them cautiously, both fish spook immediately. It's hard to get close to wary browns in shallow water under a bright sun, especially when you're wearing a flame-orange vest.

We see more fat browns as we head downstream, easily visible as they push up wrinkles of water in the shallow pools. Invariably they spook before I can get a fly over them.

As we near the reservoir, the streambank becomes softer and softer until my boots sink to their tops with every step. Then I reach a long, narrow strip of land that sticks out into the reservoir itself, with the sluggish river flowing on one side and a broad stillwater bay on the other. The little peninsula is flat and free of brush or other obstructions, an ideal casting platform, and down near its tip I can see heavy fish rising where the river blends with the reservoir. But to get there, I first have to cross a small side channel of the river.

The earth on either side of the channel is the color and consistency of chocolate pudding. That it's far too soft to support a man's weight is evident from the tracks left by others who have tried to cross; some of those tracks are so deep I wonder if the people who made them might still be down there. I take a single tentative step, and my foot, already heavily encased in mud, sinks in farther, and I am forced to withdraw in wistful frustration. Less than a hundred yards away the trout are still rolling, but they are as far beyond my reach as if they were on the moon.

On the way back I fish some of the pools we passed over on our way downstream and finally manage to get my fly over a large trout without spooking it. For some reason, though, the fish doesn't appear to see the fly—maybe the trout is blind in one eye—so I pick it up, cast again and drop the fly on its other side. The trout bolts as if someone had set fire to its tail. And that is as close as I come to hooking a fish.

Yet it's not a wasted day. What day of fishing ever is? There's plenty of wildlife to be seen along the river bottom. We jump a startled deer and see the tracks of many others, watch an otter gleefully sliding through the shallows on the wings of the weak current, observe a muskrat mucking around in its den, and flush three great blue heron. All around us are straw-colored hills covered with clots of dusty sage, and beyond them the Ruby Mountains soar to greet the season's first snow. The aspens clustered in the runoff channels are at the peak of their fall colors, and they look like ragged veins of pure gold running down the hillsides. Over everything looms the bright cobalt color of the clear October sky.

Sunday night: Back in Elko it is quiet again. The Broncos, Blazers and pickup trucks have vanished back into the hills from whence they came, leaving the streets nearly empty. The streets look dusty and a little forlorn in the early autumn twilight.

Playing the Numbers

There was a time in my life when it's possible I was even more interested in baseball than fishing. This, of course, was when I was young, and I suspect it was mostly a matter of access; it was a lot easier to find a baseball game somewhere in the neighborhood than it was to find good trout fishing, especially when a bicycle was my primary means of transportation.

My interest in the national pastime made me something of a statistical fanatic. Given the name of any major-league player, I could recite his career batting average, the number of home runs he had hit, his RBI record, stolen bases—virtually any sort of statistical trivia short of his bank account. After listening to me spout such statistics endlessly, my father began calling me "a walking encyclopedia of useless information."

The baseball infatuation was temporary, but the statistical habit turned out to be permanent; it wasn't long before I began looking for ways to adapt it to fishing. Fly fishing is a sport remarkably bereft of statistics—there are, thank goodness, no "famous fly fisher" trading cards with mug shots on the front and catch-and-release records printed on the back—but I still managed to find some things to count. I began keeping careful records of each fly pattern I used and the number of fish it caught, and at the end of the season I would prepare an elaborate statistical summary—today it would be called a spreadsheet—showing the number and species of trout taken on each fly, when they were caught, and so on.

I don't really know what I expected to learn from all this, if anything at all; it just seemed a pleasant way of keeping track of things. Or perhaps I was just hopelessly bound up in the role of being a walking encyclopedia of useless information.

Yet now, after nearly forty years of such record keeping, I'm beginning to think the information might not be useless after all. The numbers reveal some interesting changes in my angling habits over the years; they also suggest some remarkable changes in the preferences of trout—and offer some sobering food for thought.

Back in the 1960s, when I began keeping records, the figures show I caught many more trout than I do now. The statistics don't reveal the reasons, but I think there are several. For one thing, I was then still in that stage of an angler's development when large catches are more important than anything else. Also, in those days I fished exclusively for trout and hadn't yet become enamored with steelhead—something guaranteed to lower your annual catch rate. But the most important reason is that there simply were more trout then, and not so many anglers chasing them.

In those days my ten most effective fly patterns were all nymphs or wet flies. It wasn't until 1972 that a dry fly found its way onto the list. The numbers for that year also show I used fewer fly patterns than ever before, probably an indication that I was developing more confidence in my favorite flies and fishing them harder. I didn't realize it at the time, but these were trends that would continue.

The next season—1973—the figures show a precipitous decline in my trout catch for July and August, a reflection of more time spent in pursuit of steelhead during those months. Always before I had spent the late summer months fishing for trout in alpine lakes or mountain streams, but by the mid-'70s I was spending nearly all my time on steelhead rivers. That trend also would continue.

The seasonal records were fine as far as they went, but it seemed to me they didn't go far enough, so I began keeping cumulative records. That way I was able to produce a list of my all-time ten most effective fly patterns, which I updated annually. The most recent version of that list, incorporating data from nearly forty seasons, shows my all-time best flies are five nymphs, three dry flies and two soft-hackled wet flies (nearly all are my own patterns, so their names are unimportant).

For me, though, statistics are like potato chips: You can't eat just one. To satisfy my appetite, I put all the numbers on a computer so I could easily massage them many different ways. For example, I know I fished differently forty years ago than I do now, so my forty-year list of top flies is not necessarily representative of the patterns I use today—but I was quickly able to generate an up-to-date list by using the computer to slice off the data for just the past five seasons.

The results show that over the past five years, eight of my ten most effective fly patterns have been dry flies—confirmation that in forty years I've gone from being almost exclusively a wet-fly and nymph fisherman to being almost exclusively a dry-fly fisherman.

But I'm not the only one who's changed. The figures show that trout also have changed their preferences; they no longer seem interested in popular fly patterns that worked extremely well just a few years ago. Again, the statistics don't reveal the reasons, but I think it's because of the steadily increasing popularity of catch-and-release angling. Like many fly fishers, I now do most of my fishing on waters where catch-and-release is either required or common practice, and there are many more such waters now than there were a few years ago. I'm convinced that if trout in these waters are caught two or three times on the same pattern, they learn to steer clear of it. I can't think of another reason why imitations that worked faithfully decades ago now seldom take fish on the same waters.

These days I fish less often for trout than I did when I was young, and when I do my aim is not to catch lots of them but to concentrate on a few large or difficult trout. That change in habits, coupled with the fact that there aren't as many trout today as forty years ago, has meant a continual decline in my average seasonal catch. Some seasons are still better than others, but the overall trend is inexorably downward—I know, because I plotted the numbers on a graph. Yet even with a steady decline in annual numbers, over the forty years I've been keeping records I've recorded the capture and release of close to ten thousand trout.

That's a sobering number. If I can catch that many trout in a fishing lifetime, others certainly can, too—that many if not more.

What would be the consequences if we killed them all?

Think about it: If every fly fisher killed ten thousand trout in his or her lifetime, there surely wouldn't be many left; even hatcheries couldn't keep up with the demand.

So, if nothing else, my forty years of statistics seem to offer a compelling argument for catch-and-release.

I didn't have that in mind when I started, and I certainly didn't expect it to turn out that way. But if such figures can help establish the catch-and-release ethic, then they are anything but useless.

In fact, maybe it would be a good idea if everybody started keeping such statistics.

Part Two

YOU SHOULD HAVE BEEN HERE YESTERDAY

Flies were of no account among these wild fish. They had not learned the ways of a civilized state of society.

—JAMES G. SWAN, *THE NORTHWEST COAST,* 1857

Our party never caught over seventy-five fish a day . . . but easily could have taken twice the numbers.

—CHARLES H. MERRY, *AMERICAN ANGLER,* 1884

THE GOOD OLD DAYS

If fly fishers ever think about anything besides the fishing they're doing right now, it's probably about the fishing they missed. Nearly every angler has heard old-timers talk about how much better the fishing was in the "good old days," and such tales make it hard to keep from wondering just how good the fishing really was back then—or how much better it must have been even before that.

Such musings make modern anglers feel as if they were born too late. But is that really true? Was the fishing really better back in the "good old days"?

It's fun to speculate about the answer, although speculation isn't always necessary. Fly fishing has a rich heritage of angling literature that tells us what the fishing used to be like. British anglers, for example, can spend *Days and Nights of Salmon Fishing on the Tweed* with William Scrope (1843), experience *A Summer on the Test* with John Waller Hills (1924), or cast a fly *Where the Bright Waters Meet* with Harry Plunket-Greene (also 1924). They can relive the great turn-of-the-twentieth-century dry-fly-versus-nymph debates of Halford and

Skues, or sample the fishing even farther back through descriptions penned by Berners, Samuel, Walton and Cotton, to mention just a few of the seminal writers on the sport.

North American fly fishers also can turn to an extensive written history to satisfy their curiosity about what the fishing used to be like. East Coast anglers can travel back in time to fish vicariously through the words of Theodore Gordon, George LaBranche, Edward Ringwood Hewitt and other giants to learn what they missed.

So far, so good. But as we work our way farther across the North American continent, the written record of early angling grows shorter and shorter. This is to be expected, since the American West was the last frontier to be wrested from its native occupants and settled by people with fly rods and a written language.

The record is especially brief in the Pacific Northwest, where I live and do much of my fishing. Here everything is still relatively new and the first angling books did not appear until the twentieth century was already well under way. Much of the region's early fly-fishing history remains obscure.

Yet it must really have been something. Just think of it: Before the arrival of the first great waves of settlers, this great, water-rich, fish-abundant region was virtually a blank slate. There were no cities, no freeways, no strip malls or real-estate developments or dams or pollution. All the rivers still ran free under the shade of great primeval forests, and their great runs of steelhead, salmon and cutthroat had scarcely been touched. It must truly have been an angler's paradise.

But were any anglers here to enjoy it? The answer, if we dig deeply enough, is yes, there were a few, including some who fished with flies, and a few of those left written accounts of their fishing. For the most part these accounts are frustratingly brief, and sometimes almost devoid of emotion, but they still offer a tantalizing glimpse of what it was like to be an angler in the Pacific Northwest 150 years ago.

~ ~ ~

Probably the first written record of fly fishing in what was then called Washington Territory is a brief mention in the diary of James Gilchrist Swan, published in book form in 1857 as *The Northwest Coast* and republished many times since.

Swan was an interesting character. Norman H. Clark, in his introduction to the 1969 edition of Swan's diary, described him as "a moral refugee disguised as a businessman" who "found shelter and solace in the wilderness of the Northwest Coast" starting in 1852.

> He had chosen a shallow harbor [Shoalwater Bay, now known as Willapa Bay], bound by rock and sand and dark cedar forests, in a season of heavy winds and relentless rains. He was one of perhaps two dozen white Americans then on the Pacific Coast north of the Columbia River. Yet he settled there and built a cedar cabin, happily turning his back on the polite and predictable world of commerce he had left in Boston and on the larger implications of middle-class life in the United States.
>
> Learned in geography and history, trained in admiralty law, experienced in trade, elegantly schooled in social graces, Swan had nevertheless kicked against the apparently secure and rewarding circumstances of his 34 years as a proper New Englander. He had fled from a wife and two children, a prosperous ship-fitting business, and an immeasurable and forever private burden of frustration or remorse or regret.

Though Clark didn't mention it, Swan also was a fly fisher— but not, apparently, a very persistent one. His 409-page book is replete with accounts of Indian fishing methods and great catches of salmon and sturgeon, but among all this verbiage only two paragraphs are devoted to fly fishing. And here they are:

The next morning . . . I went up stream to catch trout. About four miles above our camp the stream was quite shallow, with occasional deep holes, where overhanging roots made just the shade the trout like for their hiding-places. I had some of the nicest sort of flies, of various patterns and styles, and I anticipated rare sport, but after trying half an hour without the least semblance of a bite, I returned to the canoe . . . and found the two Indians who were with me very leisurely and lazily engaged in pulling in the trout as fast as they saw fit to throw their hooks overboard.

I found that flies were of no account among these wild fish. They had not learned the ways of a civilized state of society; so, putting up my patent apparatus, I adopted the Indian plan, and between us three we caught a barrelful in about three hours' fishing.

The stream Swan fished was the Naselle River, a tributary of Willapa Bay, and the "Indian plan" to which he referred was to use salmon eggs for bait—not an auspicious beginning for the man who was probably the first fly fisher in Washington Territory. Perhaps the fishing in the "good old days" wasn't always as good as the old-timers say.

But Swan soon had company on the Northwest rivers. About the time he was finding northwestern trout too uncivilized for his flies, members of the Northern Pacific Railroad Survey expedition were working their way westward, some of them fishing as they went. The survey took two years, from 1853 to 1855, and the resulting multivolume formal report to Congress wasn't published until 1860. It included detailed descriptions of the flora and fauna encountered by the surveyors along the route, plus accounts of the incredibly abundant salmon and trout of the Pacific Northwest.

Most of these accounts were the work of two members of the expedition, Dr. George Suckley and Dr. James G. Cooper. Suckley was a fly fisher, although by no means a purist, and the report included several descriptions of his fishing experiences. Mostly, these are pretty understated, lacking any sense of excitement or discovery, and while that's a little disappointing, it is understandable, because Suckley was writing a formal report for Congress, not a story for an outdoor magazine. That's undoubtedly why his descriptions are missing the colorful adjectives we might expect from an angler who had just cast the very first fly into virgin waters.

Suckley told about fishing for a trout he identified as *Fario stellatus*, or the "Oregon brook trout" as he called it, but his description made it clear he was really fishing for sea-run cutthroat.

"While stationed at Fort Steilacoom [near modern Tacoma], I frequently amused myself by angling for trout, either using the 'artificial fly' or common bait," he wrote. "Angle-worms being not found, as yet, in that region, I was obliged to rely upon meat, fresh fish, and salmon-roe, when desirous of using natural bait."

The trout, Suckley reported, were

> found in many of the small lakes on the Nisqually plains near Fort Steilacoom, from which they can be taken in great numbers with the "fly," affording much sport to the scientific angler. The largest caught by me, in that vicinity, were taken in February from the tidal waters of a small mill-stream. They weighed a little more than two pounds each, and were the largest of the species that I have ever seen.
>
> The fish . . . were caught with a large, gaudy, *unnatural* salmon-fly. In the same stream, but from the brackish water near its mouth, I caught, in January 1854, many trout. Some were taken with the "revolving spoon," and others with the "fly," or with meat. . . . A fish, in bad condition, taken at that time, had the following colors: Back, bright olive; belly, light yellowish white; numerous black spots on head, sides and fins.

Patches, under the chin, of very pale yellowish vermilion, not bright red, as in the same fish when in good order. . . . In common with the other trout this is called the *kwuss-putl* by the Nisquallies [local Indians]. It is a fine, active trout, affording much sport to the angler.

There are several intriguing things about this account. One is that Suckley never revealed the names of the streams he fished or exactly how many trout he caught; in that respect, his report is similar to those of contemporary anglers reluctant to part with their fishing secrets. Another odd thing is that Suckley always put quotation marks around the words *fly* or *artificial fly*, as if they were unusual or exotic terms—which, in that time and place, they may well have been.

But perhaps most intriguing of all is his observation that angleworms were not yet found in the region. If true, we can only assume the pioneers hadn't yet thrown out enough coffee grounds to get them started.

Suckley also wrote of another trout, which he named *Salmo masoni*:

I obtained this species at the Cath-la-pootl River August 2, 1853, and am indebted for it to the skill of Captain McClellan, as he took it with the artificial fly at a time when they did not readily bite any bait.

When fresh its colors were as follows: Back, dark olive; sides, silvery, with green and purple reflections; belly, white; iris, yellow; spots, black. . . . For reasons that seem to me sufficiently good, I have considered this fish distinct from that described as *Salmo clarkii* by Richardson, and have named it in honor of my good friend Governor Charles H. Mason, of Washington Territory.

From Suckley's description it's obvious this trout also was a cut-throat, and it's curious he thought it was a different species from the one he caught near Fort Steilacoom—especially in view of the following statement, which he appended to his account:

> There is a trout very common in the small streams emptying into Puget Sound near Fort Steilacoom during the latter summer months and early autumn, which resembles this species very closely, and probably is identical with it. They are caught freely with either common bait or the "artificial fly" [there it is in quotation marks again] but by preference choose more readily half-dried salmon roe, which fishermen, who are not too sportsmanlike to indulge in such unartistic angling, very frequently use . . . With such bait, and with "artificial flies," the writer has taken in a few hours large strings of handsome trout, on one occasion catching 34 fish, the aggregate weight of which, when some hours out of the water, amounted to 15 pounds.
>
> A favorite place for catching these fish is McAllister's Creek, a small stream about eight miles from Olympia, the capital of Washington Territory. The best spots for fishing there are below the "old mill site" at a point where the stream meanders through the Nisqually tide prairies and where the tide ebbs and flows strongly. The best angling is had during the last of the ebb, and half through the flood, at which time the trout, having retreated to the deep holes, can be caught very rapidly. At the same place I have caught with a hook and line several young silver salmon, such as might be called by the English, grilse.

It would be difficult to find a better description of the fishing in McAllister Creek today. It's also worth noting that in this case

Suckley not only reported the number of fish he caught but also the name of the stream they came from.

The Cath-la-pootl River mentioned by Suckley, incidentally, is now known as the Lewis, and the Captain McClellan who caught the trout described by Suckley was George Brinton McClellan, later commander of the Union Army of the Potomac during the early days of the Civil War. Evidently he had better luck fly fishing for cutthroat than he did fighting Confederates.

After the report of the Pacific Railroad Survey there is a gap of nearly a quarter of a century in the written record of Northwest fly fishing. The next published account I have uncovered was a series of articles by Charles H. Merry, which appeared in a magazine called *American Angler* in 1884. Little is known about Merry other than his name, and his series of articles was terminated abruptly and without explanation after the appearance of the fifth article, leaving one to wonder if maybe the editor was getting a little tired of the whole business. Or perhaps he was growing suspicious of the information Merry was sending him, for reasons we will see a little later.

Since Merry was writing for an outdoor magazine, and not a formal report for Congress, his language had a great deal more descriptive detail than Suckley's and conveyed a little more of the sense of what it must have been like to fish in the vast northwestern wilderness:

> "From the moment you leave Astoria on a voyage outward across the Columbia River bar, you become impressed with the utter loneliness surrounding you. The tall and weather-beaten cliffs, towering above the surf and echoing back the endless roar of the waves, are as sterile and rocky as the Mexican coast a thousand miles farther south, and five times as densely timbered. . . .
>
> In the recess of Baker's Bay lies the small hamlet of Ilwaco, and there, stepping ashore from the steamboat, we leave the

Columbia River behind us, and a drive of eight miles brings us to Shoalwater [Willapa] Bay. Transferring our luggage from the wagon to a light sailboat, we cruise 12 miles northerly across a bay famed for its fine oysters, sweet clams, monstrous crabs and flat flounders. Suddenly we notice a small gap in the dense forest, and our guide, John Lane, exclaimed: "Well, fellers, here is camp at last."

But it is a long way from camp, for we sail nearly four miles up the stream against an ebbing tide, which, added to the natural current of the stream, makes our progress slow and difficult. Suddenly the muddy banks vanish, as if by magic; the clear stream crosses over a gravel bed, and a few scattered hemlocks dot the grassy meadow. Right ahead of us is a structure that the hand could never have built. It is one of the huge jams of logs peculiar to the North Pacific Coast streams. Here are interwoven and cross-laced hundreds of fallen forest giants, the towering pine and sturdy hemlock blended together in the embrace of death. This is the logjam of the Naselle River.

(The Naselle, also fished by James G. Swan, seems to have been a particular favorite among Northwest angling pioneers.)

Merry's party quickly set up camp and cooked dinner. Then, with "the frugal meal over, the younger members of the party wash the dishes while the captain of the expedition begins to joint his favorite rod. . . . He sorts over two or three books of flies and leaders, making up the casts for the younger members, and preparing for the evening's fishing."

It is a great mistake to suppose the Oregon and Washington streams require any great variety of flies. For the morning fishing, Jungle Cock, Gray Drake and Brown Hackle. . . . For evening fishing, a Coachman, Red Hackle and Gray Palmer.

Should this not prove a tempting bait, remove it and replace with a Grizzly King, Gray Hackle and Red Ant.

It is now past 4 o'clock and the sun has sunk behind the hill which rises above the big jam. Louis and Father have already disappeared over the hill, leaving Bob and myself to fish in the foaming swirls below the jam, while Lane the guide has taken his rifle and gone in search of a deer. I cross the stream to fish with face toward the setting sun, while Bob crouches in the shadow of the tall hemlocks. Before I have fairly reached my station I hear an exclamation of surprise from Robert, who has hooked his first 2-pounder. I clamber around the north side of the jam and stand with my back to a huge log, on which I can sit down whenever I feel tired. Fortunately, the sport is too exciting for any such repose. At every cast a fish of some size vaults at the lure. I have taken nine fish, none of them less than half a pound, while Bob has six, two of which are larger than any in my creel.

The sun has gone down, leaving the sky a canopy of purple and fretted gold, while the robin is chanting his vespers from the hemlock overhead. As I reel in my 16th fish, Bob reminds me that it is 6 o'clock, and he has taken 12. Returning to the campfire, I put on a fresh draft of maple wood and set on the kettle to boil. Then going down to the water's edge I clean 16 of our smallest trout, none of them less than three-quarters of a pound. Rolling them in cracker crumbs I have them ready for the frying pan when I see my father coming over the hill. In his struggle to get through the brush he has torn his pantaloons in a dozen places and his burly figure presents a laughable appearance. His misfortune ends there, for he has taken 26 fish to Louis' 18, though two of Louis' are larger.

Our three weeks on the Naselle River were three weeks of unbroken enjoyment. The woods about the camp abounded with spruce grouse, wild pigeons and deer, while a pull of four miles down the river brought us to the broad bay where we had our choice of sea food. But the real feature of the place was its trout fishing. We caught from 40 to 60 fish per day, though it was seldom that more than two were occupied. If my father asked me to accompany him trout fishing, Bob and Louis were sure to take their guns and bring home a fair supply of grouse and pigeons.

So Merry enjoyed great success fishing for trout in the Naselle River, and it seems likely he was a more accomplished angler than James G. Swan. For example, when Merry recommended fly patterns in sets of three, he meant that all three should be used at once, with one as a point fly and the others as droppers. Swan, on the other hand, may have used only one fly at a time.

After relating his experiences on the Naselle, Merry went on to tell about the fishing in scores of other Washington streams and lakes as far north as the Canadian border. He described the fishing on some of these waters in fair detail, while listing many others merely by name. But the curious thing is that after his visit to the Naselle, Merry never again wrote in the first person. His subsequent articles give the impression he was personally familiar with the waters he described, but he never once came right out and said anything to prove he had actually fished any of them.

Maybe that's why the editor of the *American Angler* suddenly canceled the series: He might have gotten suspicious that Merry was feeding him articles based largely on hearsay, or perhaps he realized that Merry couldn't possibly have visited or fished all the waters he described.

But that's merely supposition on my part, and if there is any reason to doubt Merry's veracity on other matters those doubts surely do not apply to his description of fishing the Naselle; it has the ring of truth and affords one of the best glimpses we now have of what fishing was like in Washington before it became a state.

After the appearance of Merry's articles, published accounts of fly fishing in the region remained few and fragmentary well into the early twentieth century. But as the area's population grew and the number of fly fishers grew along with it, more and more of these fishermen began to record their impressions and experiences. A few of these descriptions have appeared in print, but most have not. Among the latter are records kept by two men who surely deserve the title of Northwest angling pioneers—Letcher Lambuth and Enos Bradner.

Lambuth, a Seattle industrial realtor, was the first to collect and identify northwestern trout-stream insects and tie flies designed to imitate the naturals, but his greatest claim to angling fame was his innovative construction of spiral bamboo fly rods, which are still prized by collectors. He kept an angling diary from 1935 to 1937, and although he was known for his courtly manner and love of good conversation, little evidence of these traits is visible in his diary entries; when it came to putting his angling exploits down on paper, Lambuth always seemed to be in a hurry, and his diary often is disappointingly terse. He also had the habit of referring to himself in the third person, by his initials, B. L. L. (his full name was Benjamin Letcher Lambuth, the middle name stemming from a distant family relationship to John Letcher, Civil War governor of Virginia). Nevertheless, his diary gives a good idea of what fishing was like around Seattle seventy years ago.

Bradner became locally famous as longtime outdoor editor of the *Seattle Times* and author of several books, including *Northwest Angling*, which appeared in 1950 as the first serious work offering a full description of the numerous fishing opportunities of the region. If Bradner kept a fishing diary it seems not to have survived, but he did leave a manuscript containing what amounts to a diary of fly fishing for steelhead on the North Fork of the Stillaguamish and several other western Washington rivers in the late 1930s. It's hard to say exactly what Bradner had in mind when he prepared this manuscript. He wrote often for outdoor magazines, but he doesn't seem to have intended this piece for publication; perhaps he simply felt it was important to preserve a record of the kind of fishing he experienced.

A second Bradner manuscript described the early history of Pass Lake on Fidalgo Island in northern Puget Sound, still a popular fly-fishing destination. Unlike the steelhead manuscript, this one was clearly intended for publication in an outdoor magazine, although there is no evidence it ever was actually submitted. Both manuscripts now offer a fascinating look at some of the fishing of the past.

But let's start with Lambuth's diary. Here are his notes from a trip to the upper Skagit River in British Columbia in July, 1935:

> Left Seattle 4 A.M., arrived [border] 7:45 A.M.; American customs open 8 A.M. Around Hope 10 A.M. Arrived Camp 15 at noon; by horse, arrived Camp 29 4:30 P.M. Water high, weather very warm, moon on wane. Light and dark caddis, gray drake, candy fly, flying caddis observed. Fish reluctant; some evening strikes on Orange Caddis No. 8, and also Yellow Caddis No. 8.
>
> Took fine catch second day: 19 fish, average weight probably 1½ to 2 pounds on Dark Caddis No. 10, peacock body, brown legs, dark bucktail. About 60 fish brought out in good condition on ice. Party Joe and Chuck Black, Harold, B. L. L.; guides Tom O'Rourke, Bill Richmond. Fished entire zone of about five miles below Camp 29, very bad brush. Rates, horses $1.50 per day (six saddle, three pack), men $3.50 per day; grub, $25.

Here's Lambuth's entry for a September 21, 1935, trip to the Humptulips River, which flows into Grays Harbor on the Washington coast:

Spent Friday night Hoquiam. Left 6, arrived river 7:30, took trail 8 miles. Chum salmon in river. Water low, somewhat stained. Caught as follows: seven rainbow, 21 inches, 16 inches, 13 inches and small; four cutthroat 14 to 16 inches. Lost three hooks in fish. Yellow Caddis, Orange Caddis, dry. Returning car at 7, en route 7:30, Hoquiam 9, Olympia 10:30, Seattle 12:15. Weather warm and clear.

On July 24, 1936, Lambuth and his friend Vernon Severance fished the Green River south of Seattle. He wrote:

Special stop Lemolo. Down track one mile, fished back to Lemolo, two miles to Eagle Gorge. Train at 6:10 P.M. One of best days fishing ever had. Limit catch 9 to 14 inches. Some larger fish not held. For several hours a fish was raised on nearly every cast. Yellow Caddis No. 8 preferred; Dark Caddis and Orange Caddis also taken freely. Fine, hot day.

Despite his abbreviated fishing reports, Lambuth found room in his diary to record other things he considered important. Tucked in among the fishing entries are several pages of recipes for gin and whiskey punch. Judging from the colorful stains on these pages, the punch was thoroughly sampled before the recipes were written down.

If Lambuth was the soul of brevity, Bradner was loquacious to a fault. His manuscript titled "Summer-run Steelheading on the North Fork Stillaguamish" (north of Seattle) is full of Batman-style prose, including this account from July 15, 1937:

Deer Creek Riffle, 6:30 A.M. on a cloudy morning, with the sun coming through at 9. Water temperature 54 degrees. I covered the hole methodically with a Bucktail Coachman. No touches.

Then I bent on a No. 6 Orange Shrimp and started in at the extreme head of the run. On the second cast—wham, bang, socko, a steelhead about jerked the rod out of my hand. Not to be outdone, I jerked right back. Something had to give and it wasn't the fish. I reeled in and found the point of my Harrison hook had broken off.

Nothing daunted, I tied on my last Orange Shrimp and after only two more casts there was a second terrific strike. I didn't push that one so hard and it stayed on.

My how these Stilly sea-rainbows can run. It took out most of the tapered line on its first run and then started surface flopping out in the swift current. It wasn't big, about four pounds, and so I was able to tire it and finally got it out onto the beach. And as the fish lay there, the point of the Harrison hook snapped off. I will never use one again.

After rummaging around through the fly box I found a Bucktail Coachman dressed on a 3906 hook and tied it on. And believe it or not, hardly five minutes had gone on before I was fast to another steelhead.

Zing, on its first run, the fish took out all of the tapered line. Then it came to the surface and rubber-banded all over the river. It looked big, at least a 10-pounder. It got me so excited that I dug a trench in the gravel bar running up and down before I recovered most of the line. Then it took

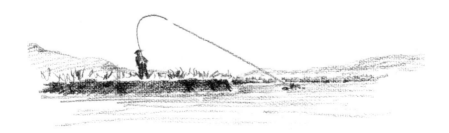

another run and got out most of the backing a second time. I did not want to lose my Halford line so released most of the pressure. The steelhead kept jumping around mostly over in the next county. Finally it rolled onto the leader and snapped off the fly.

Not a bad day, the first time I ever fished at Deer Creek. Had three on and landed one.

Thirteen days later Bradner recorded another trip to the North Fork, mentioning his now famous fly pattern, the Brad's Brat, for the first time. "About 20 feet below the lip of the riffle at the head of the hole I had a hit on a Brad's Brat," he wrote.

The fish ran upstream towards the big rock and then right at me. It made the usual long runs with surprising speed and pep. Ran into shallow water but still had lots of fight. Beached it at last, a bright four-pounder.

I waded right back into the hole and at about the third cast hooked another one. It immediately took out line and during the next few seconds jumped out of the water about 50 feet upstream. I backed up the bar, reeling madly and got most of the line back on the reel. Then the fish swam right at me and I had to reel faster than ever. Then right close to shore it jumped again right up into the air. Then downstream and out again into the current. Then it started leaping. Five times it went into the air, beautiful leaps, with me trying to lower the tip and alternately releasing line and taking up slack.

It then came into shore with fin and tail out of water. Suddenly it circled back into the river so rapidly the line bit into the water in a taut arc singing with the tension as the fish leaped again. All of this happened so fast and furious that I was worn to a frazzle and my wrist was limp. Finally it came back into shallow water, its runs shorted up and I was able to turn it on its side and beach the ironhead. Only about six pounds, but what a scrapper.

Yes, indeed. Fish just don't fight like that anymore.

Bradner also wrote about steelhead fishing on several other western Washington streams, including Canyon Creek, the Skykomish River and the Wind River, and his accounts mentioned several other well-known anglers of the time, including George McLeod, Sally Pemberton, Dr. Marvin Brown, Homer Kirby and Reuben Helm.

Bradner's Pass Lake manuscript, titled "The Miracle of Pass Lake," was written about 1950 or 1951 and described the fishing in the lake from 1939 to 1950. That Bradner wrote it with the idea of submitting it to an outdoor magazine is obvious from the opening paragraph, which is filled with the kind of outrageous hyperbole that was popular in the hook-and-bullet press of the time:

The damsel nymph fly hadn't traveled ten feet on the upward retrieve when there was a slight twitch on the line. I set the hook and with a slashing sock a silvery cutthroat trout boiled on the surface. Then it sprinted into a long run that ended in a showery jump as it shot a foot clear of the water. I was fast to one of Pass Lake's 18-inch cutts that galloped and cannon-balled with all the exhilarating abandon of a trout filled to its spotted tail with untrammeled vigor.

We had pushed out onto the mirror-like surface of Pass just as the pre-dawn mists were swirling off the water and found ourselves right in the midst of one of the lake's phe-nomenal rises. The trout were slurping all over the place, some just dimpling the surface and others rising with a deep gulp that sounded like a boot being pulled out of the mud.

That day we were surfeited with the sort of fly fishing that normally falls only to the lot of the angler who has traveled to virgin waters in the backwoods country of the far north.

With an opening like that, who could possibly resist reading the rest of the article? But just to make sure, Bradner added this:

The history of Pass Lake is so remarkable, so fascinating, so filled with enticing phases of modern trout management— ranging from the top to the bottom of the scale of success— that it should be required reading for every sportsman from the Pacific to the Atlantic. But instead it is virtually unknown outside the confines of the Puget Sound Northwest.

At various times during the past ten years fishing at Pass has ranged from nothing at all to some of the best trout angling in the Northwest. It has put out three- and four-pound trout while lakes for hundreds of miles around were producing, at their best, 10- to 15-inchers. Its piscatorial population has varied from exotic six-pound Loch Levens [brown trout], leaping five-pound rainbows, three-pound native cutthroats, down to stunted four-inch perch.

He went on to tell how Pass Lake was "discovered" in 1939 by a small group of anglers who sampled it,

and to their surprise creeled fat 15-inch rainbows which had grown from a casual planting by the [Washington] Game Department. . . . The news leaked out and the following year the lake was jammed with fishermen who caught great numbers of rainbows mainly through the use of the single salmon egg as bait.

Then in 1941 the lake was restricted to the use of the fly only, the first such regulation to be made by the Game Commission of Washington. At that time it was considered a highly revolutionary type of fish management by many western sportsmen. Moreover, it caused a great deal of opposition from anglers who felt that their rights had been interfered with.

Despite the new regulation, fishing declined over the next few years and suspicion grew that the lake had become infested with scrap fish. "Finally," Bradner related,

> the Game Department decided to poison or rehabilitate the lake. . . . In the late spring of 1946 the lake was given its dose of rotenone. Although almost 1,500 trout were killed, most of them were of small size . . . but—and here was the cause of the decline in Pass's trout population—about 500,000 undersize perch were killed. . . . These perch had consumed so much of the food supply that there was very little left for the trout.

The lake was allowed to lie fallow for the balance of the year and was planted with cutthroat trout in the spring of the following year. These fish grew rapidly and by the spring of 1950 20-inch cutthroat were common in Pass Lake, Bradner reported. He concluded the article by recalling an autumn day when, as he put it, "the trout went on a feeding rampage. They would climb onto a fly dropped near the heavy weed growths with smashing strikes that zipped line off the reel like a dynamo. They leaped often and were almost as frisky as steelhead."

Yes, there's no doubt about it, they just don't make trout like that anymore. Maybe the fishing really was better in the old days and those of us alive today will just have to accept the fact that we came along too late to enjoy the best of it.

But thanks to Enos Bradner, Letcher Lambuth, Charles Merry, George Suckley, James G. Swan and a few others who were fortunate enough to be here before we were, we can still at least vicariously share in the experience of what it was like to cast a fly into the waters of the Pacific Northwest during the first century of its recorded history.

FISHING WITH BILL NATION

Sooner or later nearly all anglers feel the urge: an intense desire to leave everything else behind and go fishing for the rest of their lives. Unfortunately, very few are ever able to fulfill that wish.

Arthur William "Bill" Nation was one who did. Nation abandoned both his native England and his profession as a pharmacist to take up a pastoral life tying flies and guiding anglers in search of Kamloops trout in the far-off lakes of southern British Columbia.

Many of those lakes were just being stocked with trout for the first time when Nation arrived on the scene in the 1920s. The trout fed avidly on the enormous natural storehouses of food in these fertile waters and grew rapidly, with some reaching awesome size. Nation established his headquarters at Echo Lodge on Paul Lake near Kamloops, right in the center of these inviting waters, and proceeded to explore the nearby lakes and learn the habits of their fast-growing trout. From this knowledge he developed a series of highly imaginative fly patterns—Nation's Fancy, Nation's Silver Tip, Nation's Green Sedge, Nation's Special, Nation's Mallard & Silver, Nation's Red,

Nation's Blue and others—that quickly won favor with local and visiting anglers and eventually became the favorites of an entire generation of Kamloops trout fishermen.

Nor was that all. Until his death in November 1940, Nation was continually involved in projects to improve the fishery. He experimented with transplanting sedges (caddisflies) and crayfish from one lake to another to provide additional sources of trout food, and came up with the idea of sterilizing trout so their growth would not be limited by spawning—a notion far ahead of his time.

Some anglers have called Nation the Pacific Northwest's answer to Theodore Gordon, the sainted fly tyer who blazed a trail for eastern fly fishers. Indeed there are some similarities: Both were bachelors, skilled fly tyers and angling innovators. But Nation's large, colorful flies are in sharp contrast to Gordon's spare, precise patterns, and unlike Gordon, a prolific correspondent, Nation left few written records of his life and work. Nation's fly patterns and experiments have been well documented, especially in the writings of Roderick Haig-Brown, but they tell us little about the man himself. We know he had an inquiring, innovative mind, but we know little else.

Who, exactly, was Bill Nation? What was he like as a person? Perhaps more relevant, what was it like to fish with him? At this distance in years, it's difficult to get a grasp on these things; the only people who could really answer such questions are those who actually did know him and fish with him, and sadly there are very few left, if any. However, it was my good fortune to hear the recollections of several of these fishermen before they departed to fish in uncharted waters.

From these accounts, plus the written remembrances of others who knew him and Nation's few remaining letters, I have pieced together a scenario of what it might have been like to spend a day or two fishing with him in the mid-1930s, when he was at the peak of his reputation. True, it has been necessary to fill a few blank spots in the narratives I've gathered, but I think the following account is as accurate as it can be, considering the lapse of more than six decades.

So come with me now and let's enjoy a couple of days fishing with Bill Nation:

The time is late June 1935. You've just arrived in Kamloops by train, which is by far the fastest, most convenient way to reach this outpost in the remote British Columbia interior. By prior arrangement, someone from Echo Lodge is waiting at the station to meet you and load your baggage into a wood-sided station wagon for the trip to Paul Lake. Even though it's only twelve miles, the drive takes about an hour because the road, still years shy of its first pavement, is wet and slippery after recent rain.

It's early afternoon when the station wagon finally pulls up under the shade of the trees around Echo Lodge and J. A. and Vivian Scott, the proprietors, step outside to welcome you. They quickly show you to your quarters, make sure you're settled comfortably, invite you for tea, and tell you what time dinner will be served in the lodge dining room. And finally, that evening, when dinner is over, comes your long-awaited introduction to Bill Nation.

His appearance surprises you a little. He's not a big, rugged, outdoor type, as you might have expected; instead, this man who put Kamloops trout fly fishing on the map is small and slender and looks rather like someone who spends most of his time writing tedious sums in thick ledgers. His large, horn-rimmed glasses give him something of a scholarly appearance, and his long hair is parted a little to the right of center and combed straight out on either side in the fashion of the day. Only his dress—an old sweater worn over a faded shirt and faded trousers—plus the ruddy marks of sunburn on his face, give evidence that this is a man who spends most of his life outdoors.

His manner at first is diffident, almost shy, and you find it hard to believe this is the famous guide you've heard so much about. But he wastes no time getting down to business: Speaking softly, he asks to examine your tackle, and you take your rods out of their cases and hand them over. Of course they are all made of cane, because nothing else was available then, and Nation looks them over with a practiced eye, joins the sections together, flexes each rod in the air, and finally pronounces himself satisfied.

Then he asks to see the flies you've brought along, and when you open your fly boxes he shakes his head and says, "These will never do. But no matter; I have plenty of my own, and they are guaranteed to kill."

Next he asks for your reels so that with the help of one of the other guides—Jack Morrill or Alex Vinnie—he can unspool the braided silk lines and stretch them between a pair of trees overnight so they will be ready to fish in the morning. Finally he asks for your "casts," or gut leaders, and takes them to soak overnight in a pail of water so they will be pliable enough for fishing the next day, when you will carry them in round tin cases lined with water-soaked felt pads. Today we'd think these things a terrible bother, but back then they were simply what you had to do in order to get ready for fishing, and you did them as a matter of course.

Next morning, after a leisurely breakfast at the lodge, Bill would go through his own little ritual of consulting the barometer, by which he set great store. You're in luck; the reading is favorable. If it were otherwise, he might have declared it useless to go fishing that day, and nothing you could have said or done would have persuaded him to change his mind.

Next he would help you rig up your rods and then lead you down to one of the big old Clinker-built wooden rowboats at the lodge dock. Since there would be no insects hatching early in the day, he would likely start you fishing with one of his famous attractor patterns, such as the Nation's Special or Nation's Fancy. When he was satisfied the fly was tied properly to the end of your gut leader and everything else was ready, he would take the oars and steer the boat along the edge of a shoal.

The shoal's outline would be easily visible through the clear water, and Nation would suggest that you cast either into the shallow water over the shoal or into the deeper water beyond it, depending on where he thought the fish would be feeding.

The Nation's Special would soon stir up a fish or two, each a bright, lively two- or three-pound trout that Nation would land by hand, since he never used a net or a gaff. Yet these would be only a warm-up for what would come later, when the sun finally came full upon the water and the sedges started to stir. Then Nation would tie on one of his Green Sedge patterns, or—if he thought your casting left something to be desired—he might tactfully suggest switching to his Green or Gray Nymph, which he would tell you imitated dragonfly nymphs, and have you trail one behind the boat while he rowed. He might also offer you a casting lesson, for by all accounts he was an expert instructor.

As the hours passed and he grew more accustomed to your presence, Nation's shyness would disappear and he would begin to talk animatedly. Mostly he would talk about fishing—and not just the fishing at Paul Lake, but also at the nearby Adams or Little Rivers, or at Peterhope or Hihium or Devick's Beaver, or other places, perhaps even Taupo or Rotorua in New Zealand where he sometimes guided in the off-season.

The mention of Little River would really get him going. "It might be the most interesting fly fishing in the world," he would say. "You can see all your fish, as they are a quarter of their depth out of water, and tell their size and condition, and you must solve the problem of being able to spot the fly just in front of their noses. Use a line greased all the way to the end, and a twelve- or fourteen-foot leader greased halfway, and a light Mallard and Silver number 2 fly. If the fish are upstream, cast just below them, about nine inches, and let the fly come downstream unchecked about three feet, then lift and recast. Strike at the splash; the least drag is fatal."

He would talk also about the insects in Paul Lake and other nearby waters, the sedges, damselflies, dragonflies and chironomids, and explain their habits and how they moved in the water, and why it was so important to imitate those movements closely with an artificial fly. He would tell about his efforts to tie flies that resembled the naturals, about the materials he used and all the effort it took to get them, and how he had to order many of them from Allcock's, Hardy Brothers or Veniard's in England, and wait weeks for their delivery through the mail.

He might explain how the light changed a little each day, and how those changes affected the reflective qualities of his flies, and how he varied their construction and materials to account for those differences. Sometimes the shape of the fly would need changing, too, he would say, but this could be done merely by a little "scraping or biting."

Whatever he talked about, it would serve you well to pay close attention, because in those days Bill Nation was practically the sole source of information on fly fishing for Kamloops trout. There were no books on the subject then, no classes or clinics or seminars, no videos and no Internet, and information was hard to come by. But information was Nation's stock in trade: He had invested the time and made the observations necessary to learn more about the fishing than anyone else, and if you wanted to share in that knowledge you had to spend time with him, listen carefully and watch everything he did. That was the only way.

Yet fishing wasn't all he talked about. As he grew more at ease with you, Nation's impish sense of humor would begin to assert itself. He might gently ask if you happened to be of Scottish descent, and if you said you were not, then he might poke a little fun at the expense of Scotsmen. One of his favorite things was to ask if you knew why Scotsmen wear kilts, and if you made the mistake of saying no, he would explain it's because they are all born with tails, and kilts give

FISHING WITH BILL NATION

them more freedom to wag their tails when pleased, or lash them when angry, or tuck them between their legs when in retreat. He seemed to think Scotsmen were easy targets for humor, much the same as "Newfies" (Newfoundlanders) are treated nowadays.

On the other hand, if you said you *were* of Scots descent, then Nation might invite you to join the Research Foundation of Canada, a tongue-in-cheek organization he claimed to have founded for the purpose of refuting all the ancient "calumnies aimed at Scotsmen." He would gladly accept your five-dollar membership fee, as long as you understood that one of the basic precepts of the organization was that the treasury would never be audited.

He would have you laughing as well as catching fish long before the day was over. And while his jokes might have been of the catch-and-release variety, you probably would have kept all the fish you caught without feeling guilty about it because the idea of releasing fish was virtually unknown in those days. And when you returned to the lodge, if you wanted a fish for dinner, Nation would select one and turn it over to the chef. He would take the others and clean them, which he would do by removing their gills first, then withdrawing the rest of their innards through the resulting cavity; that way it was never necessary to cut the belly of the fish, so it would be intact for mounting if that was what you wanted to do with it. When you were ready to leave, he would pack the fish in boxes between layers of moss covered with ice, and these would be taken to Kamloops and sent home to you by railway express.

On the second morning of your trip, you would travel by horseback to a remote lake high in the hills. Nation would carry your fly rods in an old golf bag attached to his saddle, and his horse would lead the way up the trail. Your horse would follow, and if you were not accustomed to riding horses you would probably enjoy the experience for a while, until the steady motion began to rub you raw in some delicate portions of your anatomy.

Your discomfort would quickly be forgotten when you came in sight of your destination: a shining lake hidden in thick timber, with only a single little log cabin and a leaky old rowboat to indicate that you were not the first persons ever to visit. Nation would bail the boat while you got ready for fishing, then he would take the oars and row you out onto this strange and inviting water.

Later you wouldn't remember going ashore for lunch, nor would you remember that it had rained a little in the afternoon. You would not even remember the growing discomfort of the downhill horseback ride in the gathering twilight. And the reason you would not remember is because the fishing was so spectacular it crowded everything else from your mind. The trout were huge—at least six pounds on average, perhaps as much as eight, with some weighing even more: great, shining, husky trout that stripped enormous amounts of line from your reel and leaped to unbelievable heights. Never before had you experienced fishing like this, and you could hardly dare hope that you ever would again.

Of course you didn't land all the fish you hooked—you might not have landed even half of them—but each was a separate adventure in itself, a wild sequence of blurred line and flying water, fast-running reels and shouts of exultation. Together they merged into a vivid series of memories that you would carry all the rest of your days.

Next morning, all too soon, it would be time to leave Echo Lodge and return to the railway depot in Kamloops for the first leg of your long journey home. When your bags were safely stowed in the station wagon, you would say your farewells to Mr. and Mrs. Scott and Bill Nation. You would already have settled your account with Bill—ten dollars for two days of guided fishing, plus another dollar for flies—but you might also want to slip him an envelope with a generous tip, say an extra five dollars, just to show your appreciation for the wonderful time you'd had. Or, like some of his other clients, you might want to wait until you got home and then send him a book inscribed with a few words of appreciation.

And you would always remember Bill Nation as one of the most remarkable men you had ever met.

And that is why we still remember him today—because of who he was, and all the remarkable things he did, and for everything he means to the history and heritage of fly fishing in the Pacific Northwest. It's true his fly patterns and his ideas today no longer occupy center stage—they've gradually been superseded by newer patterns and fresher ideas—but that is the natural way of things, and disuse is not a synonym for disrespect. Nation's works have now passed into the realm of angling tradition, and tradition is important because it helps define who and what we are. It is also something that requires constant nurturing, and by writing and reading about Nation we continue to nurture his part of our angling heritage.

What would Nation think about all this if he were still here among us? I imagine he would be a little surprised that people are still writing and talking about him, but not greatly so; despite his humble manner and his simple lifestyle, I have the sense that he was a man of more than ordinary self-esteem who had a pretty good notion of the significance of the things he did and of his place in history. Yet while he might not be surprised, I think he would still be immensely pleased that we remember him, and still honor his contributions.

But what of the future? Will the next generation of anglers remember Bill Nation? They will if we continue to perpetuate the tradition, if we keep his name alive and his memory fresh. I sincerely hope that will happen, and that perhaps in another sixty years anglers will still be writing and talking and thinking about the life and times of Bill Nation, and what it was like to fish with him.

REMEMBERING RALPH WAHL

I t's hard to realize I may now be the last survivor of all the anglers who fished with Ralph Wahl. From Ralph, one of the great pioneers of steelhead fly fishing, I learned more about the sport than from all other sources combined. It was Ralph who guided me to my first steelhead and to many others that followed, and I always considered it a privilege to fish in his company.

I knew him all my life. He was in the same Bellingham, Washington, high-school graduating class as my parents, and many years later one of his sons was in mine. As a boy I remember going into Wahl's Department Store in Bellingham and seeing him there, an imposing figure in a formal suit. I also remember sitting through many lurid Westerns at Bellingham's old Grand Theater while Ralph ran the projector (his family owned the store and theater).

Perhaps it was because of these early connections that Ralph took me under his wing many years later when I began fishing for steelhead, and that was when we really became friends for the first time. He soon guided me to that first steelhead, taking me to the place, showing me which fly to use and telling me exactly where to place the cast. A fish came to the fly, just as he had assured me it would, and at the moment it felt the hook, I felt it, too—and I have been hooked on steelhead fly fishing ever since.

Ralph and I fished together many times after that, often for steelhead but sometimes for trout. We usually went in Ralph's camper; he would drive while I rode shotgun. He was a quiet man and I tend to be that way myself, so we never said very much on these trips. We would either sit in comfortable silence or listen to some of the remarkable tape recordings Ralph had made: the awesome chorus of an endless flight of sandhill cranes passing over Peterhope Lake, conversations with Northwest fly-fishing giants such as Tommy Brayshaw and Roderick Haig-Brown, or seminars at some of the early conclaves of the Federation of Fly Fishers. Some of the latter were intensely interesting—some, but not all, and more than once I dozed off to the monotonous drone of voices from the past.

When we got where we were going and set up camp I would always get a little nervous because Ralph was a very fastidious man; everything in his camper had a specific place and there was a specific place for everything, and if you didn't know where something belonged and put it in the wrong spot you were sure to incur his displeasure. He would rarely say anything about it, but his body language was very clear and left you in no doubt that you had screwed up. I was always relieved when breakfast was over and the dishes had been washed and put away—each in its own very particular place—and we could go fishing.

Ralph was the most accurate fly caster I have ever seen. Even at a great distance or in a nasty wind, he could place his fly exactly where he wanted it nearly every time. It was an ability I envied, although I remember one occasion when something distracted him and he didn't notice that his fly had landed on a log. As he started gathering line the hook caught momentarily in the log's bark, then popped free and fell in the water. Ralph felt the momentary resistance and exclaimed: "There! I had a strike!" I smiled and said nothing; it was simply proof that even Ralph was human.

He coached me carefully and passed along many tips and suggestions, not as a teacher lecturing to a student but simply in a matter-of-fact, straightforward manner that was easy to accept and remember. I could not have asked for a better mentor; Ralph had been fly fishing since 1925—the first fish he caught on a fly was a three-pound cutthroat—and for some years he held the Washington State record for the largest steelhead taken on the fly, a twenty-and-a-half-pound winter fish from the Skagit River. He was known throughout the land as one of the Pacific Northwest's most accomplished steelhead fly fishers.

The lessons he taught remain vivid many years later, and I continue to follow his advice religiously. It has paid dividends many times, with only one exception: I remember Ralph emphasizing the importance of getting your fly under a logjam whenever possible, because steelhead will often hold under the shelter of the logs. I've done that faithfully at every logjam I've ever encountered, but I don't recall hooking a single fish that way. Still, I expect to keep doing it and have no doubt the day will come when that piece of advice also will bear fruit.

Ralph usually remained carefully in control of himself, but he did have a temper and if provoked sufficiently he would sometimes lose it, occasionally with spectacular results. One such incident occurred on British Columbia's Roche Lake. Ralph had anchored his boat near an island and was casting outward into deep water when another fisherman came by in a motorboat, trailing a gang troll—a long string of flashy revolving spoons. The other angler steered right through the water Ralph was fishing, and Ralph had to strip in his line quickly to prevent it from being cut by the outboard motor or caught in the gang troll. Ralph did so without saying a word.

The other fisherman kept going for some distance, then turned around and came back through the water Ralph was fishing, forcing him to strip in his line a second time. Still Ralph said nothing. The troller continued to the end of his beat, made a U-turn and came back again. Ralph retrieved his line once more, still maintaining his silence, although even from a distance you could feel his blood pressure rising.

Finally, when the other fisherman returned for the fourth time, Ralph—still without uttering a word—suddenly double-hauled, shot a cast toward the other man's boat, and planted his fly squarely in the back of the goose-down jacket the other angler was wearing. Then Ralph tugged hard on the line until the fly popped out in a great explosion of goose feathers.

When the other angler realized what had happened, he throttled up his outboard and sped away as fast as he could. Ralph calmly resumed fishing as if nothing had happened—and there was no evidence that anything had, except for a big patch of goose feathers floating on the surface of the lake.

Ralph was noted as the author of a number of fly patterns, including the Lord Hamilton, Lady Hamilton, Winter Fly, Paint Pot and Wahlflower. But I rarely saw him use any of these patterns; he had others, not so well known, that he used more frequently. Some had been developed for use in specific situations or places, and they worked with great success. One in particular worked so well that I tied copies for my own use, and it still works well today—although, in keeping with Ralph's well-known reputation for reticence, I'm not going to describe it.

What about that reputation for reticence? It grew out of the fishing reports Ralph used to give as a longtime member of the Washington Fly Fishing Club. He would introduce himself as "Ralph Wahl from Bellingham," then proceed to describe amazing catches without ever revealing exactly where he had been fishing or what fly he had used. This went on for years, until the club finally presented him a gadget with an arrow on its face that could be dialed to point to a word describing the fishing Ralph had experienced—GOOD, BAD, or INDIFFERENT—so Ralph wouldn't have to say anything at all. The device even had a leather thong so it could be worn around his neck.

It was meant as a joke, of course, but Ralph showed up at the next club meeting wearing the gadget around his neck, and when it was time for fishing reports he announced himself as "Ralph Wahl from Bellingham," turned the arrow until it pointed to GOOD, then sat down without saying another word.

The truth of the matter was that although Ralph had many angling friends, he shared his secrets with very few of them. Some people resented this reluctance to reveal his favorite spots or the dressings of some of his favorite flies. Perhaps they failed to realize the effort it had taken him to find those places or develop those patterns—a great investment of time, toil, sweat and maybe sometimes even tears. When you have paid such a price it teaches you the value of things, and I understood Ralph's reluctance to share his secrets with others who had not paid the price. He was generous with me because I knew what these things had cost him, and because he knew I would value them as much as he did—and keep my mouth shut.

Even though Ralph is now gone and many of his favorite spots are gone, too—victims of the ravages of time, nature and "progress"—I still try to protect the identities of the few I know are left. Partly this is out of respect for Ralph, but mostly it comes from concern for the fragility of these places in a world that seems bent on squeezing the best from everything. These sacred waters don't belong exclusively to me, however, so I have shared them with a few other anglers whose discretion I trust. It will be up to them to guard Ralph's secrets when I am gone.

Like many people, Ralph sought a means of expression and found it in photography, a hobby he combined with fishing. He started working in color but discovered he could capture more feeling in black and white. He looked for scenes where anglers appeared as small, insignificant visitors in the great cathedral of the outdoors, and many of his photos reflect this vision. He had a true artist's eye for composition, a way of seeing to the heart of every scene, and his remarkable darkroom skills brought each image to sensitive fruition. The result is a wonderful photographic legacy of a Northwest most of us are too young to have known—vistas of great, gray unfettered rivers flowing under great, gray unblemished skies; clear, swift torrents bordered by ancient stands of timber towering into mist; snow-speckled winter riverscapes and bright fish fresh from the sea. His photos appeared in *Time* and *Life* magazines and numerous outdoor publications, and during my years as editor of *The Flyfisher* magazine, I published many of them inside the magazine or on its cover.

Ralph's photographic work also was on display in the basement of his Bellingham home, a treasure trove of angling history. His "rogue's gallery"—photographic portraits of many of the twentieth century's most famous anglers—brought visitors from far and near.

Ralph's first published work was an article on winter steelhead fly fishing that appeared in a national outdoor magazine in 1943, helping establish his reputation as a pioneer of the sport. Years later, in 1971, he published his first book, *Come Wade the River*, which included many of his best photographic images matched to selected excerpts from the text of Roderick Haig-Brown's classic *A River Never Sleeps*. The book now is a collector's item.

A second book, *One Man's Steelhead Shangri-La*, published in 1989, is an account of one of Ralph's secret spots, a slough at the mouth of Day Creek on the Skagit River, describing the wonderful steelhead fishing he experienced there. He felt safe revealing the location because by the time he wrote about it the place had long since been destroyed by floods. I felt honored to be asked to write the foreword for the book, and a copy of the original typescript, autographed by Ralph, is one of my most treasured possessions.

The wear and tear of old age forced Ralph into a wheelchair for the last several years of his life, but he bore these circumstances with little complaint. He spent his last days surrounded by his fishing books, tape recordings, photographs, memories and friends. He always kept a box of flies near his wheelchair—the last flies he tied—and pressed several of them into the hands of nearly every visitor. The last time I saw the box, just before Ralph died, it was nearly empty.

I visited him often during those last days because we were working together on a fly-fishing exhibit at the Whatcom Museum of History and Art in Bellingham. Many of Ralph's photos had been selected for display, and he was enthusiastic and excited at the prospect. He was looking forward to the exhibit's opening, which seemed to give him a reason to keep going—that, plus his oft-stated wish to outlive his old angling friend Enos Bradner, who had lived to age ninety-two.

But it was not to be. Ralph passed away June 4, 1996, at age ninety, just a short time before the exhibit was due to open. The museum dedicated the exhibit to his memory and named it after the title of his first book, *Come Wade the River*.

When that book was published, Ralph told friends it was his "monument." In truth, it was only one monument among many—his wonderful photographs, his fine words on paper, his wisdom on recording tape and his own legendary place in the steelhead fly-fishing traditions of the Pacific Northwest.

In May 1969, when the Washington Fly Fishing Club celebrated its thirtieth anniversary, Ralph was among the featured speakers, presenting an oral "fishing report" spanning the entire history of the club. His conclusion: "The fishing has always been poor."

I knew when he said it that he was joking—because if you were lucky enough to be with Ralph Wahl, the fishing was always good.

Part Three

CAUSES AND CONTROVERSIES

Women fishing is one thing, and watching women fishing is another. But women watching fishing—well, in my experience, women who watch fishermen . . . almost invariably remind me of a dog watching television. They have no capacity of sustained attention, no concentration whatsoever, and an eye only for the extraneous and inconsequential.

—ARNOLD GINGRICH,
THE WELL-TEMPERED ANGLER, 1965

It is a scientist's privilege to change his mind.

—DR. DAVID STARR JORDAN, QUOTED BY BEN HUR
LAMPMAN IN THE COMING OF THE POND FISHES, 1946

SENSITIVITY TRAINING

I confess I am prejudiced. I am partial toward trout, steelhead and salmon and prefer them over all other freshwater species, especially bass, bluegill, crappie and other warm-water fish.

It's not that these other fish don't have their place; obviously they do—just so that place isn't where *I'm* fishing. Usually that's somewhere in my native Pacific Northwest, which also is native country for trout, steelhead and salmon. Bass, crappie and bluegill also have been introduced throughout the region and have managed to survive and thrive in its warmer lowland lakes and ponds, but that doesn't mean they *belong* here. To me they are ecological invaders, like starlings or cheatgrass—at best something to be tolerated, at worst a nuisance.

At least, after a lifetime of fishing for trout, steelhead and salmon, that's how I feel about it. But I'm aware there are a lot of other anglers who feel otherwise. They tell me I really don't know enough about bass and panfish to recognize their virtues, and perhaps they're right. I've always been so intent on fishing for indigenous species that

I've usually avoided waters holding non-native fish. Only rarely have I encountered bass and panfish, and then mostly by accident.

My first meeting with largemouth bass was in a little lake that in an earlier life had been a millpond. The mill was long gone—a victim of cut-and-run logging tactics—but its concrete foundation was still visible beneath the shallow waters of the pond. Also visible were some of the logs that never made it to the mill, now jammed into the bottom muck at crazy angles or stuck against the shoreline in tangles of brush. A splendid crop of lily pads grew up on all sides of them. I suppose it was good habitat for bass, but it wasn't bass that drew me there; I'd heard the pond harbored some large cutthroat.

My very first cast was taken by something that felt like a small weed had attached itself to the fly. It turned out to be a largemouth bass about the size of my thumb, and at least a third of that size was mouth. More fish of similar size followed on almost every cast, and it was obvious the bass had gleefully reproduced until they were far too numerous for the carrying capacity of the small pond; they had become stunted as a result. This is a frequent outcome of bass or panfish

introductions in the Northwest; somebody should talk to these fish about family planning.

But there were still cutthroat in the pond, and the bass made nice, kibble-sized treats for them. I put on a Muddler Minnow about the size and shape of the tiny bass—and just large enough that the bass couldn't wrap their mouths around the hook—and caught some heavy, healthy cutthroat.

So that was my introduction to the largemouth bass: Not as a game fish, but as food for trout.

Later I ran into them again in an unnamed desert pond whose surface was speckled with impressive rises. Thinking the rises were caused by feeding trout, I quickly began casting from shore and soon had a heavy take that turned out to be a fat, foot-long bass. It fought well, but gave up in less than half the time it would have taken to subdue a trout of similar size. Other bass followed, almost too easily, until I soon grew tired of catching them and went elsewhere to look for trout.

I first ran into bluegill in a forest pond where I'd gone looking (as usual) for trout. The colorful fish were a novelty at first, and it was amusing to watch them rise and take a floating moth imitation—but even with a light rod, I had to be careful not to set the hook too firmly or the little fish would come flying right out of the water. That's how small they were.

Several years ago the television show *Northern Exposure* aired an episode in which Dr. Joel Fleischman, one of the show's leading characters, hooked a leviathan-sized fish that towed him far out onto a fog-shrouded lake, where he somehow ended up in the belly of a whale. I happened to know the location of the private lake where the episode was filmed, and also who owned it. I'd also heard that it harbored cutthroat not much smaller than the whale that swallowed Dr. Fleischman.

After some negotiating, my son Randy and I obtained permission to fish the lake, and on the appointed day we went there with high hopes. The lake *did* hold cutthroat, but the largest—caught by Randy—turned out to be only fourteen inches, and most were much smaller. We also found zillions of bluegills, each about the size of a fifty-cent piece. Their numbers and gluttony undoubtedly helped explain the small average size of the cutthroat.

I've since found bluegills in other waters, but never any larger. I hear they grow bigger in their native waters, and perhaps under those circumstances they provide better sport. But not around here.

I guess my attitude toward crappie is best summed up by what my old friend and fishing partner Ed Foss used to do to them. Ed liked to fish a lake near Tacoma that held fat trout, and sometimes I would join him there. The trout rose well to hatching chironomids in the fall, but the lake also had a burgeoning population of crappie that likewise enjoyed sipping chironomids, and it was impossible to avoid hooking a crappie now and then. Whenever Ed caught one, he'd unhook it, yell "Frisbee!" and see how far he could sail the dinner-plate-shaped fish across the lake. He achieved some impressive distances, too.

Of course I've encountered these fish in other waters, but never under circumstances where they've impressed me as being remotely comparable in sporting quality to trout, steelhead or salmon. I hear there are some local waters where largemouth bass grow hefty enough to offer a real challenge, but I've not been tempted strongly enough to try any of them.

The smallmouth bass has a reputation as an outstanding game fish, and although smallmouths are present in some local waters I've yet to try them. Several of those waters are on the list of places I intend to fish, but the number of untried trout and salmon waters still ahead of them is large and it probably will take me a long time to work my way down to the smallmouths. I'll reserve judgment until then.

I mean no disrespect to those who prize bass, crappie and bluegill as worthy fly-rod opponents. If I lived where these fish are native I suspect I would feel the same way. But I live in the Northwest, and I don't understand how other anglers who live here can prize these other fish more than our indigenous species. Mostly, I suspect, they are people who moved here from elsewhere and brought their angling preferences with them.

Those who harbor such preferences tell me I'm missing something, that I'd surely gain more respect for the sporting qualities of bass, bluegill and crappie if only I'd spend a little more time fishing for them and get to know them better. In other words, they hint— none too subtly—that my bias against bass and panfish might be cured by a little sensitivity training.

Perhaps so. But with so many trout waters yet to fish, and so many salmon and steelhead rivers yet to explore, I'm afraid my sensitivity training will just have to wait.

WIVES AND LOVERS

It happened during one of the early conclaves of the Federation of Fly Fishers. Ed Zern, the late outdoor humorist, had badgered the master of ceremonies all through the proceedings for a chance at the microphone, insisting he had something very important to say. Finally, at the concluding luncheon, the master of ceremonies called Zern to the speaker's platform and told him to go ahead and say whatever it was he was so anxious to say.

Zern took the microphone in hand and said: "Ladies and gentlemen, my topic today is sex. It gives me a great deal of pleasure."

Then he sat down.

I think it also was Zern who once complained that "whenever I go to my fishing club, all they ever talk about is sex, and whenever I go to my sex club, all they ever talk about is fishing."

Well then, since this is a book about fishing, how could it not have a chapter about sex? Or, in this case, about fly fishermen's wives and lovers, which is pretty close to the same thing?

You might reasonably ask why this subject should be included in a section about "Causes and Controversies." The answer is that whenever the topic of wives or girlfriends comes up in conversations among male anglers, certain highly controversial questions are bound to arise. For example: Should wives, or women in general, be permitted to attend fly-fishing club meetings? Should they be allowed to attend club outings? Should they even be granted the privilege of accompanying their husbands or significant others on fishing trips? These issues never fail to generate heat, sometimes plenty of it.

That being so, it seemed to me a prudent idea to see what others have had to say about this subject before venturing any opinions of my own. This prompted an extensive review of angling literature, which revealed, somewhat disappointingly, that the subject of fishing wives and girlfriends was almost totally ignored by angling writers until the beginning of the twentieth century, and it hasn't exactly been a hot topic since.

Of course, we shouldn't overlook the fact that the very first fishing book in the English language is credited to a woman, Dame Juliana Berners, although there is some doubt she really was the author—and even if she was, she had nothing to say about fishing wives. That's to be expected; as prioress of an English abbey, Dame Juliana obviously was unmarried herself. Her treatise is filled with good advice about closing gates, not breaking down hedges, and other bits of wisdom, but on the subject of domestic relations in a fishing family she was completely silent.

From her time until the twentieth century fishing apparently was pretty much a man's game, even as it mostly still is today, and the men who wrote about fishing didn't see fit to say much of anything about their wives or girlfriends, if they had any. But early in the twentieth century some stories about the wives of fishermen began to appear. One of the best, and best known, was titled "A Wedding Gift," by John Taintor Foote.

The hero, a man named George, married a woman named Isabelle late in life and took her fishing in Maine on their honeymoon. After a series of misadventures, he succeeded in hooking a huge, legendary trout known as Old Faithful. And this is George's story:

At last the fish began to come. He wasn't tired—he'd never done any fighting, as a matter of fact—but he'd take a suggestion as to where to go from the rod. I kept swinging him nearer and nearer the cove each time he came around. When I saw he was about ready to come I yelled to Isabelle. I said, "I'm going to bring him right past you, close to the top. All you have to do is net him."

He was a little leery of the cove, but at last he came. I steered him toward Isabelle and lifted him all I dared. He came up nicely, clear to the top. I yelled, "Here he comes! For God's sake, don't miss him!" I put everything on the tackle it would stand and managed to check the fish for an instant right in front of Isabelle.

And this is what she did: It doesn't seem credible—it doesn't seem humanly possible; but it's a fact and you'll have to take my word for it. She lifted the landing net above her head with both hands and brought it down on top of the fish with all her might!

From that, you will get the idea this marriage was not exactly starting off on the right foot. If you want to find out how it all turned out, you'll have to read the story, which is perhaps the most amusing of its kind in all of angling literature.

Another famous story is "The Lady and the Salmon," by Andrew Lang. It's not exactly a story about a fly fisherman's wife because the couple in the story never did get married, although they came close. It seems that on the morning they were to be wed, the groom-to-be hooked a mighty salmon and fell into the river in an unsuccessful attempt to land it. He arrived at the church dripping wet and forty-five minutes late for the ceremony, and the bride-to-be walked out in a huff. As any good fly fisherman would tell you, this was extremely unreasonable behavior on her part, and it's probably fortunate the groom found out what sort of woman she was before he took the final, fatal step.

The late Corey Ford once wrote a story called "Trout Widows." The gist of it is summed up in the first two paragraphs:

> The papers were filled with the details of the Twitchells' divorce last week. You may have noticed it, because it was rather an unusual case. All the wife did, according to the story, was to send her husband's felt hat to the cleaner. "Absolutely all I did, your honor," she explained to the judge in filing suit on the grounds of desertion, incompatibility and cruel and unusual punishment, "was just to take this dirty old hat that he'd been wearing for years, with grease stains all over it and the top crushed in like a muffin and the hatband practically ripped to pieces where he'd kept trout flies in it, and sent it around the corner to be cleaned and blocked. And then he came home, and took one look at it, and began smashing the furniture and throwing it at me, and setting fire to the house in several places."
>
> I know the husband in this case pretty well, as it happened. His name was Herbert Twitchell, and he was as mild-mannered and considerate a chap as you would ever want to go fishing with. He belonged to the Mayfly Club on the Beaverkill, and he was one of the most popular anglers on the stream. I never saw him lose his temper when his backcast caught in a balsam, or a heavy shower came up just in time to spoil the evening hatch, or when he got pebbles down inside his waders.

So once again you see what happened. A well-meaning wife, ignorant of the ways of fly fishermen, drove her usually good-natured husband beyond the point of no return. One can hardly blame him for reacting as he did, and he was probably thankful his wife sued for divorce and saved him the trouble of doing so.

The late Arnold Gingrich, publisher of *Esquire* magazine, had more experience with wives than most of us, having gone through three or four. In his book *The Well-Tempered Angler* he summed up the experience of one of his marriages like this:

> Eight months for a marriage is short even by today's standards. And it would be an oversimplification to say that, but for fishing, that marriage might have lasted longer. Still, it might not be too wide of the mark to apply here the words with which General Sarnoff has been credited: "Competition brings out the best in products and the worst in people." I keep hearing about happy fishing couples . . . who not only fish together but keep talking about meeting other people who do too. I can only conclude either that one member of the happy couple must be a liar or, if not, that they must have in equal parts the disposition of angels and the patience of saints.

Gingrich's view is decidedly pessimistic, but you might expect that of someone who was married as many times as he was.

The late Robert Traver wrote more about fishermen's wives than anyone else. I suppose it's only a coincidence that he also wrote *Anatomy of a Murder*. He referred to wedlock as "that uneasy state of truce known as marriage," and on the subject of women fishermen in general, whether married or not, he had this to say: "Women fishermen: Avoid them. One kind will quietly outwit you and generally get in your hair while another variety will come down with the vapors and want to go home just when the rise gets under way. Avoid all of them like woodticks."

Analyzing the reasons men go fishing, Traver said:

At this late hour I don't want to go in over my waders and
poach on the preserve of psychiatrists. Thank heaven I have
never been encouched and so am not qualified to do so. But
sometimes I wonder whether the wild urge to pursue and lure
a fighting fish isn't connected somehow with the—er—sexual
urges of the fisherman himself. My, my, I've up and said it!
Many frustrated and neglected wives of fishermen will doubtless rise up at this point and shout hoarsely, "*What* sexual
urges?" Hm, let us see, let us see. . . .

Under the beneficent glow of our present pale tribal cus-
toms, courtship and marriage can get to be, so my runners in-
form me, a pretty drab and routine affair; and I divine as
though in a dream that some men there are among us who
doubtless rebel at constantly laying siege to an already con-
quered citadel; and unless they are going in for collecting
blondes of assorted shades and varying degrees of moral recti-
tude, fishing and all that goes with it may be the one pursuit
that permits them to vent their atavistic impulses and still preserve the tatters of their self-respect.

An interesting theory, but also one that seems to leave little
room for cordial understanding between life partners.

Nick Lyons, in a book bravely called *Fishing Widows*, also tack-
led the question of the tension between fishermen and their wives.

Fishing is *complexly* irrelevant, and its very capacity to absorb
men completely makes it the more valuable to them—and the
less intelligible to women. A woman may not like the idea of
a mistress, but another woman is something she can understand and fight. Fishing—unintelligible and irrelevant to the

uninitiate—is, as the wise Judge Robert Traver [quoted above] wisely notes—worse than adultery.

The very intensity of the passion—often private, occasionally even religious—is of course what creates fishing widows, and I doubt if the strange predicament of the women, the frequent chauvinism of the men, can be understood or appreciated without some disclosure of how deeply the fisherman's passion runs.

Mine's unfathomable.

So there you have some insights on the subject of women and wives from some of the more discerning male members of the fly-fishing fraternity. Without exception, they view fly fishing as an obstacle to a successful marriage or relationship, or vice versa, and the literature reveals few if any examples of writers who have taken an opposite view.

That these writers knew whereof they spoke is borne out by my own experience with a number of younger anglers who have sought my advice on how they might persuade nonfishing wives to acknowledge their compelling need to get out on the water and cast a fly, and to do so often. I'm afraid my advice has never been very helpful, however, for in each case I have offered the opinion that the question of a man's need to go fly fishing is something that should be settled *before* matrimony, not after. After is too late. And by any measure, the best way to settle the matter is to choose a mate who goes fishing herself.

I can testify to that. My wife, Joan, used to fish even before we met, so fishing never has been an issue between us. We spent most of our honeymoon at a remote British Columbia fishing cabin with no running water, no plumbing and no electricity (although the place did come equipped with plenty of mosquitoes). Our marriage survived not only that but also the time she left the butt section of my favorite bamboo rod on the roof of our car and we didn't discover it missing until eighty miles later. We're still together after more than forty years, and I'm still fishing.

Of course not everyone is fortunate enough to find a bride who likes or understands fishing. Even so, I think it may sometimes still be possible for a fly fisherman to have a happy, long-lasting relationship with a nonfishing wife or significant other. They need only seek inspiration from the example of . . . a fish.

Specifically, the anglerfish. In a charming little book called *The Life Story of the Fish: His Morals and Manners*, Brian Curtis described the unusual mating habits of this fish:

> The female is 40 inches long, her devoted husband four inches long—only one one-thousandth of her weight. This species lives at great depths, in complete blackness. Its numbers are few. The chances of a male finding a female are poor, and of his losing her after he has once found her, good. What he does, then, if he has the good luck to find a mate, is to make sure that he will never be separated from her. He takes her by the throat or the back, or some other portion of her anatomy. His jaws sink in. And he never lets go again. By and by his skin grows together with her skin. Her blood vessels make connection with his blood vessels. His mouth degenerates and becomes functionless. He becomes literally one with her.
>
> Of unswerving masculine devotion to a single spouse, this is unquestionably the world's outstanding example. Here is conjugal faithfulness carried to the ultimate degree. Here are no puny words about "till death do us part." Not even death will part this little fish from his mate. If she dies, he at once dies also. Here is marital fidelity beyond the powers of the most virtuous of the human species.
>
> Poor fish, indeed!

With that sort of example, it seems fly fishermen ought to be able to get along with their wives or girlfriends, and vice versa. It will also help if they keep in mind that the pleasures of fly fishing are best when shared, and a common love for angling and the outdoors is something that should bring couples closer together rather than drive them apart.

So—Robert Traver's advice notwithstanding—take your wife or significant other with you next time you go fishing. At the very least, she'll then know for sure you're chasing fish and not something else. And she'll be able to see firsthand just how much fun you're having. She might even want to join in.

Who knows? You both could end up having a good time.

FISH CULTURE

The first time I ever heard the term *fish culture* it evoked a mental image of a bunch of fish dressed up in white ties and tails, each with a musical instrument, all busily playing Schubert's *Trout Quintet*. But I soon learned what the term really meant; it is, in fact, a euphemism—a term intended to make something seem better or more important than it really is. For although *fish culture* in its broadest sense embraces many activities, it usually means fish farming, or raising fish in hatcheries.

There was a time, of course, when everybody thought that was a good idea. Hatcheries were considered the cure for many ills; if a watershed was ruined so it could no longer sustain native trout populations, that was no problem; we could just manufacture trout in a hatchery and dump them in to replace their extinct wild counterparts. We could even make a lot more of them than nature ever could.

That sort of approach led to what is called "put-and-take" fishing, and for years that was the norm in fisheries "management." All you had to do was raise as many trout as possible to a catchable length of six inches, then release them somewhere—anywhere—so people could "harvest" them.

It wasn't long, though, before some anglers—fly fishers in particular—began questioning the put-and-take approach. They were more interested in catching a few large trout, preferably wild, than hundreds of naive little liver-fed cookie-cutter hatchery fish. Unfortunately, they had trouble making themselves heard. I can remember once standing in front of the state fish and wildlife commission and asking its members if they thought the public would be pleased if the state released hundreds of thousands of six-inch deer for hunters to shoot. But the point seemed lost on the commissioners.

Now I understand why. With all the money the state had spent on hatcheries, it had a vested interest in their continued operation. Same for the people who worked in them; raising fish was how they made their living, and anyone who didn't like it was perceived as a threat to their livelihoods.

For those reasons alone, the idea of put-and-take fishing has been slow to die, even though we know now how much damage it has done, compromising the genetic integrity of countless wild trout populations or causing their extinction through competition and displacement.

Even in the light of such knowledge, the idea of raising fish and planting them is still attractive to many people, and not all of them have a vested interest in hatcheries. For example, raising fish is an easy thing for clubs and organizations to do. It makes their members feel good, makes them feel as if they are doing something important for the resource. And state fisheries-management agencies are inclined to let them do it—who wants to turn away a group of enthusiastic volunteers? So now, in addition to the state-run hatcheries, there are countless little backyard fish-raising and -stocking operations going on.

Some of these are undoubtedly useful, while others probably just contribute to the problems caused by past hatchery and planting practices. Some are just downright strange.

I know of one club that asked the state for permission to use Vibert boxes—slotted plastic boxes that protect eyed trout or salmon eggs until they hatch—to plant steelhead eggs in the tributary of a major river. Glad for the help, the state even provided the eyed eggs, and the club members duly turned out in waders with shovels and rakes, loaded the boxes with eggs, and buried them in the gravel of the tributary.

All but one boxful, that is. One of the organizers of this effort—I won't mention his name because I think he still feels a little guilty about this—decided to try a small experiment on his own. He took home a Vibert box full of several hundred steelhead eggs and put it in the flush tank of his toilet, just to see if the eggs would hatch. Each time the toilet was flushed, the eggs got a fresh shot of oxygenated water, and after a few weeks there were several hundred steelhead alevins swimming around in his flush tank.

At a loss as to what to do next, the intrepid experimenter decided to flush the toilet one more time, and all the little steelhead went down the sewer. As far as I know, none ever returned as an adult.

Fish culture sometimes involves other activities, like marking fish raised in a hatchery so they can be identified later, after release. With trout, this usually means clipping a ventral or adipose fin. Now they have machines that will do this work, but that wasn't always the case; it used to be done by hand, and it was hard, tedious work. But that was another area where volunteer groups could help, and I have personally taken part in several such efforts.

One in particular comes to mind. It was a large-scale operation at a state hatchery, involving volunteers from a number of different fly-fishing clubs, and we had something like twenty thousand cut-throat trout fingerlings to mark in a single day. Dip nets were used to pluck fish out of the hatchery raceways and place them in tubs filled with an anesthetic that was supposed to immobilize them. But some of the fish got smaller doses of the anesthetic than others, and they were still squirming and wriggling violently when we picked them up and tried to make them hold still long enough to snip off a tiny ventral fin. Not easy, believe me.

After we had worked all morning, there was a break for lunch. Somebody had brought a couple of coolers full of beer, and along with grilled hamburgers, everyone had at least one beer—or, in some cases, two or three. Or more. Then it was back to clipping fins.

If you think clipping fins on squirmy trout fingerlings sounds tough to begin with, try it sometime after you've had two or three beers. By the end of the afternoon, some of the most grotesquely mutilated trout you ever saw were swimming feebly in the hatchery raceways; they looked as if they'd been run over by a lawn mower. It's hard to tell who felt worse the next morning—the mutilated trout, or all those fin-clipping fly fishers who'd had too much to drink.

Fortunately, not all fish-cultural efforts turn out quite so badly. In truth, hatchery-raised trout sustain many fisheries in lakes or ponds where natural spawning is impossible, and hatchery-reared steelhead have established "artificial" runs in several rivers that lacked them before. So hatchery fish can and do play a legitimate role in management when they are stocked where they are needed, with careful consideration for other species, the carrying capacity of the water, and the quality of fishing expected. In other words, fish culture isn't necessarily always bad.

Nevertheless, when it comes to culture, I think I'd rather listen to Schubert.

BOOB TUBES

One day my friend and fishing partner Dave Draheim was fishing northern California's Davis Lake when he heard a sudden cry for help. A nearby angler had suddenly noticed an alarming hiss of air escaping from his float tube. He was a long way from shore and it was obvious he would never make it before his leaking tube ran out of air. So he started hollering for assistance.

Humanitarian that he is, Dave immediately went to the rescue of the other angler, hauled him into his boat and took him safely to shore. A friend of the other fisherman witnessed the rescue and was so grateful he offered Dave a Cuban cigar as a token of thanks.

Not long after that incident, my son Randy and I were fishing Corbett Lake in British Columbia when I heard Randy shout, "Somebody's in the water!" Sure enough, a fisherman out in the very center of the lake had flipped his float tube and was hanging upside down in the water, apparently in imminent danger of drowning. Randy, who was closer than I was, began rowing frantically toward the spot, but another angler got there first. At the risk of swamping his own small boat, the other angler allowed the distressed fisherman to crawl over the transom and took him ashore.

The rescuer in this case was an angler named Richard Becker. That evening I saw Becker at dinner, told him about the Cuban-cigar episode and asked if the fisherman he rescued had given him any token of thanks.

"Yeah," Becker said. "He went into town and bought me a bottle of maple syrup. Maple syrup! I guess that was the only thing he could think of to get."

Hmmm. If I were the one who had been rescued, I think it would have been worth at least a fifth of good single malt and a whole fistful of Cuban cigars. But I don't expect ever to find myself in such a predicament because you will never catch me fishing from a float tube. Not only do I consider them unsafe, but I think they make fly fishing much more difficult than it needs to be.

Yeah, I know; I don't have much company in that view. Float tubes have become nearly ubiquitous among stillwater fly fishers all over the country. Some people are even foolish enough to use them in rivers or tidal waters.

For proof of their popularity, I need only recite my experience when I returned recently to a once favorite trout pond I last fished about fifteen years ago. The pond is a small, shallow, weedy crease of water that lies in a rocky cleft about three-quarters of a mile from the nearest road, a distance I had always considered both a blessing and a curse—a blessing because it kept angling traffic to a minimum, a curse because it was hard work to carry in the small boat I used to fish the pond. Float tubes were still fairly uncommon when I started fishing there.

The last time I had fished the pond, I would have considered it a busy day if I saw half a dozen other fishermen. I suppose it was naive to expect things would be the same when I returned, but nothing could have prepared me for the shock I received when I climbed over the last ridge and looked down at the pond.

More than two hundred fishermen, nearly all in float tubes, were jammed into less than fifteen acres of water. It looked like a bowl of Froot Loops. Anglers were kicking frantically to avoid running into each other, screaming at one another and dodging to avoid errant backcasts. Their fin-clad feet had kicked up so much silt from the bottom of the shallow pond that the water was stained a dirty shade of brown. Not surprisingly, no trout were being caught; if any remained, they were hunkered down to avoid the monumental ruckus going on overhead.

Such nightmarish scenes have become all too common. Mostly they are due to the great increase in the number of fly fishers everywhere, but this particular nightmare was due at least as much to the amazing popularity of float tubes. They have proliferated unbelievably in a short time, and now the sound of portable foot pumps echoes from the margin of nearly every trout lake, bass pond and bluegill tank in the land.

There's no mystery behind this. From their first appearance, float tubes were hailed as a convenient, lightweight, affordable and portable means of angler transportation, the perfect solution for fishing off-road lakes and ponds, a low-cost alternative to cartop boats and prams. But instead of using them only for off-road fishing, some anglers began using them for *all* fishing, and others followed suit in lemming-like fashion.

This is not the first time fly fishers have climbed onto a bandwagon without giving any critical thought to the consequences. Usually little harm is done when this happens, but in the case of float tubes the consequences can be severe—not just for personal safety, but also in terms of angling effectiveness and environmental damage.

Some of the limitations of float tubes are obvious, if trivial. For example, getting in or out of the water in a float tube is, at best, an awkward ritual that makes a fisherman look like a ruptured duck. You also must be a contortionist to change fly lines or do the double haul in a float tube, and it's not even worth thinking about trying to put on your rain jacket without making a trip ashore. Same for answering a call of nature; you might as well figure on subtracting half an hour from your fishing time. Yet many anglers seem willing to put up with these inconveniences.

But float tubes have other disadvantages that aren't quite so obvious, and some are beginning to create serious problems for both tubers and their fellow anglers. One is a subtle phenomenon that threatens to erode the traditional fly-fishing code of etiquette.

A basic precept of that unwritten code is that every angler is entitled to his or her own space, enough room to fish comfortably with a reasonable chance of reaching undisturbed fish. To a lake or pond fisherman, this space usually is a circle whose radius is a little beyond the angler's maximum casting range. Most experienced anglers know this, for they also cherish the privacy of their own space, and intuitively respect the "bubble" of fishing territory around their fellow fly fishers.

But when float tubers hit the water, this traditional respect rapidly breaks down—not, usually, from any malicious intent on the part of the tubers, but rather because a float tube provides such a low vantage point that it severely distorts an angler's ability to judge distances accurately. We're all so accustomed to gauging distances from a normal standing height that our brains don't readily adapt to a vantage point only a couple of feet off the water. The result, to an angler sitting in a float tube, is that nearby objects frequently appear much farther away than they actually are.

This didn't matter much when float tubes were still uncommon, but now that they threaten to become as numerous as mosquitoes it matters very much indeed. The reason is that the float tuber's distorted distance perception frequently causes him to stray unwittingly within the hitherto respected territorial "bubble" surrounding other fishermen. The tuber may think the next guy is a hundred feet away when he's actually only a little more than half that distance, and when one tuber innocently kicks his way into another angler's space the result is often an angry confrontation that leaves both parties seething.

A big part of this problem, of course, is again attributable to the sheer numbers of fishermen on our waters; with so many anglers, some territorial clashes are inevitable. But the problem is greatly exacerbated by the difficulty of judging distances from a float tube, plus the fact that many tubers don't even realize such a difficulty exists. The great majority of these fishermen undoubtedly are polite and considerate, with no desire to cause problems for their fellow anglers, and if they knew how their distorted perception unwittingly causes them to violate the traditional rules of angling etiquette they would probably be ashamed of themselves.

It also doesn't help that float tubes can only be navigated in reverse, which means people using them can't see where they're going, and many forget to turn around often enough to avoid blundering into another angler's fishing space.

Another problem with float tubes is potentially far more serious. It has to do with their inappropriate use. There are places where the use of a float tube is definitely *not* appropriate. These include the shallow, weedy areas of ponds or lakes where it is impossible to paddle in a tube without kicking up great clouds of silt. The resulting turbidity not only has an adverse effect on the tuber's own fishing—probably much more than he realizes, given the limitations on his vision already described—but if he kicks up too much silt or is joined by other tubers doing the same thing, it soon ruins the fishing for everybody.

All that silt suspended in the water also has to go somewhere, and eventually it sinks down into the aquatic vegetation on the lake bottom where it smothers the eggs, larvae and pupae of aquatic insects. When you consider how much silt can be kicked up in the course of a whole season by float tubers in a shallow lake, it's easy to understand how this can lead to serious long-term declines in the lake's insect hatches, which in turn results in smaller trout and poorer fishing for everybody. Fly fishing depends on having flies available to imitate, but the heavy and inappropriate use of float tubes has unquestionably harmed the fishing in many fragile, shallow-water environments.

Any angling practice that interferes with other fishermen or poses a threat to the resource will have to be regulated sooner or later, and if more fly fishers don't learn to use tubes responsibly then it's probably only a matter of time before we will see regulations limiting or banning tubes from some waters.

But those are only a couple of the subtle downsides of using float tubes. There are others.

One of the things that makes fly fishing so exciting and rewarding is the visual aspect of the sport: the chance to see and cast to individual feeding trout, then watch them take the fly. True, not all lakes and ponds are clear or shallow enough to permit this type of fishing, but many are—and float tubes make such fishing impossible. An angler sitting only a couple of feet above the surface has no chance of seeing cruising fish at any distance.

This is obvious when you think about it. Most fly fishers are well aware of the trout's so-called window—the cone-shaped area of surface visible to a trout cruising below. When the trout is at depth, the cone of visibility is large and the trout can see insects hatching or floating on a large area of the surface. But as the trout rises closer to the surface, the cone shrinks proportionally until only a small area of surface is visible. What most fishermen don't realize is that the same thing applies to them: If they are standing in a boat, well above the surface, they can see a large area beneath the surface (assuming optimal weather and lighting conditions and a good pair of polarized glasses), but if they're hunkered down in a float tube, their cone of visibility isn't much larger than the diameter of the tube itself.

This means float-tube fishermen are necessarily limited to fishing blindly, using the old "chuck-and-chance-it" method. As a result, most of the time they end up fishing water where no fish are present, which is extremely inefficient to say the least. If they were above the water far enough to see cruising fish, then they could make nearly every cast count.

Of course that doesn't prevent float-tube fishermen from casting to rising fish. But here again float tubes offer an inherent disadvantage.

Feeding trout cruise very rapidly in lakes, and fishermen must get their fly over a rising trout *right now* to have any chance of catching it. For several reasons, that's often difficult, if not impossible, to do from a float tube.

One reason is that float-tube anglers must necessarily use a long fly rod just to keep their backcasts from striking the water and ruining the cast. Long fly rods require a long casting stroke, which takes more time than is the case with shorter rods, and that extra little bit of time is often critical in a situation where every fraction of a second counts.

Not only that, but tubers are pretty much limited to covering rises within a small arc directly in their front. If a trout rises off to one side, or behind the angler, it will be long gone by the time the tuber can maneuver into position to cast toward the rise.

Perhaps these limitations are one reason many float-tube anglers cast only now and then, if at all. Perhaps without realizing it, they have become trollers instead of fly fishers, kicking merrily along in the chancy hope that a gullible trout will eventually see the fly dragging behind them. This might be a legitimate way of fishing, but it robs anglers of most of the pleasures of the sport and keeps them from developing the skills needed to become really proficient fly fishers.

Don't get me wrong, though; it's not that I believe float tubes are totally without virtue. As noted previously, their portability makes them good for fishing off-road lakes or ponds, so long as you're prepared to swim for it if you should start to hear that telltale hiss of escaping air. They also cost somewhat less than cartop boats or prams, although by the time the necessary accessories—swim fins, neoprene waders, and so forth—have been purchased, the difference isn't that great. For anglers who are willing to accept their limitations and inconveniences and use them appropriately in appropriate circumstances, float tubes may represent an acceptable solution to the need for a stillwater fly-fishing platform.

But give me a small, lightweight fishing pram or skiff any day. Such craft are extremely maneuverable and extremely safe when handled properly. They provide an excellent, high-off-the-water vantage point from which to see individual cruising fish. They also allow a fisherman to cast in any direction without having to change position, and they permit the use of shorter rods with tighter, higher-speed casting strokes to put the fly over rising trout in the shortest time possible. Finally, they allow the user to keep a proper, respectful distance from other anglers, change lines, put on foul-weather gear, answer calls of nature, or do any number of other things without having to go ashore, and they do no damage to the environment.

What more could you ask? Case closed.

THE *SALMO* SOCIETY

Starting right now, I'm accepting applications for membership in a new society. It will be called the *Salmo* Society, and its single purpose will be to change the generic name of rainbow, steelhead, cutthroat, golden, Gila and Apache trout from *Oncorhynchus* back to *Salmo*.

There are all sorts of reasons for doing this. Perhaps the most obvious is that *Salmo* is a smooth, rounded word, one that perfectly fits the streamlined shape of these noble fish, and one which—from many decades of past association with western trout—immediately brings to mind the image of a sleek, bright fish, one beautifully matched to its native environment, designed by nature to breach the strong flow of great rivers. *Oncorhynchus*, on the other hand, sounds like a noise you'd make after inhaling a snootful of ragweed pollen.

How did this happen, anyway? How did the western trout suddenly go from *Salmo* to *Oncorhynchus*, lumped in with and indistinguishable from the rest of the Pacific salmon family? In case you weren't paying attention at the time—and few anglers were, because they weren't invited to the meeting—a group called the American Society of Ichthyologists and Herpetologists, which assumes for itself the power over such things, decided on the basis of new research that a name change was in order. Obviously an outfit that calls itself the American Society of Ichthyologists and Herpetologists has no business naming anything (its members' children probably answer to names like Herkimer and Ethelbert), but the American Fisheries Society's Committee on Names of Fishes nevertheless went along with its recommendation and made the name change official.

The Fisheries Society's committee did say it "has not endorsed these changes lightly, for it has an overriding interest in the stability of fish names." If so, then it should have considered the effect of the change. It has left us with a situation in which Atlantic salmon are still classified as true trout, *Salmo*, but are commonly referred to as salmon, while steelhead are now classified as Pacific salmon, *Oncorhynchus*, but are commonly referred to as trout. How can anyone make sense of that?

Maybe all the confusion would be justified if the new research had provided definitive evidence that rainbow and cutthroat trout and their close relatives clearly belong to the Pacific salmon family. But the evidence—based on morphological, biochemical and ecological studies—is arguable and subject to interpretation, to say the least.

One of the few findings cited specifically by the researchers had to do with post-spawning survival. Always before it was believed that while some steelhead survived to spawn more than once, Pacific salmon never did. However, the researchers argued that the number of steelhead that survive spawning is not all *that* great, while in some stocks of Japanese cherry salmon, *Oncorhynchus masou*, a few individuals *do* survive after spawning. So they concluded the dividing line was not so clear after all.

But that was before recent reports from Russian biologists that 75 percent or more of the steelhead returning to Kamchatka rivers are repeat spawners. So take that and stick it up your *Oncorhynchus*!

Of course anglers are aware of many other differences among cutthroat, steelhead and Pacific salmon that probably weren't considered by the taxonomists. I have nothing against salmon, especially if there's one on the other end of my line, even more especially if it's a chrome-bright, sea-run coho; but one of the things that clearly separates salmon from steelhead is that the former lose their brightness very quickly when they enter fresh water, and by the time they have gone a little way upstream most of them are as dark and rusty as an old maple leaf. Their ruddy sides bloom with pasty-white patches of fungus, and they take on the appearance of aquatic lepers—ragged, ugly fish that look as if they might fall apart before they get where they're going. If something like that rang your doorbell in the middle of the night, you'd call 911. Steelhead, on the other hand, keep their brightness long after they enter the rivers, and thus remain desirable to catch.

That's one big difference. Another is that salmon are much more numerous, which makes them something less of a prize than steelhead, and during the brief time they are still worth seeking in rivers they usually occupy water that is far less interesting to fish than the riffles and runs where steelhead hold. Salmon migrations also are more narrowly defined by seasons than those of steelhead, at least a few of which run in every month of the year, which makes steelhead more readily available to anglers.

But the most important difference of all is the willingness of steelhead and cutthroat to take a fly, especially a dry fly, compared with any Pacific salmon. I've caught many salmon on dry flies in salt water and a few on floating lines in rivers, and I have even heard of rare occasions when someone hooked a salmon on a dry fly in a river, although I've never done it or seen it done myself. However, such occasions, when they do happen, are surely the exception rather than the rule, for after salmon enter rivers their custom is to refuse dry flies steadfastly, and often to refuse flies of any kind. This, in my opinion, is crude behavior for a fish. Rainbow, steelhead and cutthroat, by contrast, rise enthusiastically to dry flies wherever you find them. Their behavior is genteel and refined; salmon are just boors. For that reason alone, I believe fly fishers will always consider rainbow, cutthroat and their near relatives more enlightened fish than salmon, even if the latter theoretically represent further progress on the evolutionary scale.

The whole issue of generic names really boils down to a chicken-and-egg question: Should rainbow and cutthroat be classified for what they are, or for what their descendants, the salmon, have become? Just where do you draw the line? Aside from the "morphological, biochemical, and ecological" evidence—which really isn't that clear—how about drawing the line over the differences that anglers readily perceive?

That's what we'll do as members of the *Salmo* Society: We'll wage a guerrilla war against the tyranny of *Oncorhynchus* and emphasize the differences that favor changing the generic name of rainbow and cutthroat back to *Salmo*. In countless thousands we'll march on state capitals and Washington DC chanting, "Salmo! Salmo! Salmo!" and waving placards signifying our devotion to the name. We'll print

bumper stickers saying SALMO—NOT THAT OTHER WORD! and plaster them all over our vehicles. We'll also print little gummed labels saying SALMO that can be peeled off and stuck over ONCORHYNCHUS wherever it appears in books and magazines. We'll spray-paint SALMO graffiti on every wall.

And when the American Society of Ichthyologists and Herpetologists meets again, we'll be there in endless ranks, carrying our fly rods at shoulder arms, shouting all the reasons *Salmo* should be restored to its former glory as the only proper name for rainbow and cutthroat trout.

We will, won't we?

Part Four

MEMORIES ARE
MADE OF FISH

*The perversity of fish can be likened, I think sometimes, to the
perversity of cats. They won't come when you want them, but
only when they're good and sure that it's their idea and not yours.*

—ARNOLD GINGRICH, *THE JOYS OF TROUT*, 1973

*Out of the water he rose again like a rocket—out and out, and
still there was more to him, no end to him. More bird than fish
he seemed as he hovered above the water, his spots and spangles
patterned like plumage.*

—WILLIAM HUMPHREY, *MY MOBY DICK*, 1978

OPENING DAZE

April is the month when trout season opens in many states. Opening Day can be a pretty big deal if you care about such things, and there was a time when I did. I not only cared, I was obsessed; Opening Day was circled on the calendar months in advance and the date was burned into my memory. I yearned for it, dreamed of it and trembled with excitement over the prospect that at long, long last that magic sacred day would free me from an interminable gray winter of troutlessness.

Of course I was young then and hadn't yet learned about fishing for winter steelhead or sea-run cutthroat, so Opening Day held the promise of a chance to fish after months when I could only think about it. I went around saying things like "Only sixty-four more days until Opening Day" until my wife grew tired of it. "I wish you'd stop saying that," she said one day, so I did. But I continued silently calculating the number of days left until I could go fishing once again.

In those days there were a lot of rituals associated with Opening Day. I would spend much of the winter perusing mail-order fishing catalogs, a vicarious form of window-shopping, and now and then I would actually even order a few things from one or more of them. I would also make repeated trips to the local fly shops to stock up on tying materials, although this was really just an excuse to trade fish talk with the clerks and other customers.

For a week or more in advance of Opening Day the newspapers would be filled with columns discussing prospects for the season opener, listing waters by name and the expected size of the trout to be found in them. I would study these as if they were holy writ and marvel how the newspapers' outdoor editors could be so omniscient about such things. It was only much later that I learned they were merely rewriting handouts from the state game department.

Pre-Opening-Day sales were another part of the ritual. The beginning of trout season was then almost as much of a merchandising event as Halloween or Valentine's Day is now, and all the stores advertised cut-rate prices on rods, reels, lines, waders and other accessories. The ads were almost as much fun to read as the outdoor columns and the catalogs, and it was a good time to buy new tackle or replace older items that had worn out.

Naturally there was also plenty to do to get ready. No matter how many times I had tinkered with my tackle through the winter I would take it out and tinker with it yet again, cleaning and oiling reels, tying new leaders, replacing worn rod guides, inventorying flies. There were never enough flies, so I would get out my vise and tie flies far into the night, imagining each new pattern hooked firmly in the mouth of a heavy trout.

Opening Day itself always was on Sunday, much to the despair of legions of clergymen. On the day before, members of the Washington Fly Fishing Club, to which I belonged, would gather for their

Opening Day outing at Pass Lake on Fidalgo Island, another annual ritual. We would grill steaks, bake potatoes, toss salad and have a glorious dinner together, then sit around the campfire afterward swapping tales and sipping Vince Sellen's marvelous and deadly hot buttered rums.

The next morning those without serious headaches would go fishing.

The fishing was never good. The lake always was too crowded and the weather and the water were always too cold for the trout to be doing much of anything. Often it rained, and once it even snowed. But we always made the effort anyway, and it didn't really matter whether we caught anything because Opening Day represented a kind of freedom for us, a parole from the prison of winter. The calendar might say the year began on January 1, but for us it didn't really start until Opening Day.

Those were good times, but they were not necessarily good for the resource. Opening Day routinely brought out at least half a million anglers of all kinds, and that many fishermen inevitably took a grim toll of trout. Of course most of the trout were from hatcheries and had been planted expressly for the occasion anyway, but so many were caught on that first day that few were left for anglers who wanted to keep fishing after Opening Day. The crowds also created traffic jams and pollution, and those problems seemed to get worse every year. Opening Day gradually began to lose its luster, and it was obvious that changes were in order.

Those changes have long since been made. Fisheries managers, belatedly recognizing the problems of Opening Day, gradually set new seasons, weaning the crowds away from their opening feast. Many waters are now open year-round and others are opened on staggered schedules so there really isn't a single Opening Day anymore. As a consequence, the newspapers pay far less attention to the event than they used to; likewise for the merchants. Even the Washington Fly Fishing Club's annual Opening Day party has quietly gone by the boards. The crowds are no longer as bad as they were.

As for me, having grown older and presumably wiser, I now understand that Opening Day—or what's left of it—is the very worst day of the year to go fishing. I no longer get excited about it, no longer circle the date on the calendar or count the days leading up to it; now I consider it a good day to spend quietly at home, away from the crowds, the pollution and the slaughter of trout. Plenty of time for serious fishing later.

I don't regret the changes; they have all been for the better. But I do still fondly remember those earlier, somehow simpler times when Opening Day loomed as large as Christmas on the calendar, when we all seemed to have more innocence and enthusiasm than we have now, when I was still young and the sport was new and fresh.

Then Opening Day tugged at my heartstrings.

THE BEAVER-POND
BROTHERHOOD

I started fishing beaver ponds when I was young and still learning how to cast. Most of the ponds I fished were well beyond the nearest road and it took quite a hike to reach them, so there was never anyone else around to witness my casting ineptitude. To my way of thinking, that made them good places to practice.

Now, many years later, I realize that beaver ponds were *not* the best places to practice casting; most are so full of standing snags and other obstructions they can cause trouble even for expert casters. Yet they were and are good places to learn how to fish. Small and shallow, they are inhabited by wary trout that demand a quiet approach and a careful presentation. You either learn these things or you don't catch fish.

Those wary, demanding trout are one reason I still enjoy fishing beaver ponds, although there are plenty of others. In my backyard, on the wet side of the Pacific Northwest, beaver ponds have their own peculiar haunting beauty. Under dark, rain-swollen skies they glisten like obsidian; during rare moments of sunlight their acid-stained waters light up with the color of strong bitter ale. They exude a scent of mustiness and decay that's perfectly in character with their gloomy aspect. Skeletons of drowned fir, cedar and hemlock rise from their muddy bottoms like dark stalagmites, gesturing with spectral, moss-draped limbs. Great blue herons stalk these waters, ospreys nest in their tallest snags, and swallows and bats come to feed on their hatching insects.

So do trout. Some ponds hold rainbow or transplanted eastern brook trout, though the bright spots and speckles of the latter are usually sullen and subdued in the dark beaver-pond water. A few ponds hold coho salmon in the fall, resting briefly from the rigors of their upstream spawning journey. But the most familiar inhabitant of Northwest beaver ponds, the fish for whom such places seem especially to have been made, is the cutthroat.

Perfectly at home in these cluttered, hard-to-reach waters, the cutthroat prowls narrow passageways between flooded thickets in search of damselfly nymphs or hatching mayflies in the spring, then rises to capture flying termites, craneflies or almost anything else in the fall. Even in dark water these fish are neon bolts of olive, crimson and silver, glowing as if from some mysterious inner source of light. Beaver-pond cutthroat always look happy to be where they are.

Fishing in these ponds can be wildly unpredictable from one season to the next. Sometimes you will go back to a favorite pond and find it isn't even there anymore; the beaver have been trapped out or fled, their untended dam has washed away, and what was a pond last season has this year become a meadow. Even if the pond is still there, the fishing will depend on whether the season has been merely wet or even wetter than usual, whether the beaver have faithfully tended their structures, whether the trout have been successful in their spawning.

Sometimes you will find a pond that holds many small trout and the fishing will be fast and easy. Occasionally you will find one with no fish at all and end up wondering why you spent the time and effort to make the long hike in. Once in a while—just often enough to make it worthwhile—you'll come across a pond that holds a few large old trout, perhaps the last survivors of a population trapped upstream when beaver built the dam to make the pond. These places can offer the best fishing of all, though it can be maddeningly fascinating and maddeningly frustrating by turns, sometimes both on the same day.

Devices like float tubes had yet to be invented when I started fishing beaver ponds. We used inflatable rubber rafts instead—"two-man" rafts they were called, although two men would have to be very small and know each other very well to occupy one of them.

Even with only a single passenger the rafts weren't very maneuverable, and in the snag-filled waters of beaver ponds you had to be wary of splinters lying just beneath the surface—because if you hit one it could result in a ruptured air chamber and you'd suddenly be left clinging to only half a raft. The rafts weren't very comfortable, either, because if it rained—as it nearly always did—the rainwater would collect inside the raft and it would fill up like a floating bathtub, leaving you nearly as wet as if you'd fallen in.

It was a peculiarly masochistic kind of fishing. At the end of a day you'd have lost at least half a dozen flies and tippets to the ubiquitous snags and you'd be wet, weary and covered with mosquito bites. Maybe you'd have caught fish and maybe not, but you'd be absolutely certain of one thing: You had really been *fishing*. None of this wimpy stuff with guides manning the oars, chilled bottles of wine and grilled lamb at streamside; we're talking tough, do-it-yourself, hairy-chested fishing. That's what it takes to join the brotherhood of beaver-pond anglers.

A few beaver ponds reach the status of major impoundments. In one of my favorites, many generations of beaver have worked to construct a long, serpentine dam across a shallow basin, backing up enough water to flood twenty-five acres or more. Despite its size, the pond is only about four feet deep and choked with waterlogged brush, fallen timber and standing snags. Wreathed in morning mist, it's a ghostly, mysterious place, a good spot for a Halloween party any day of the year. But I love it.

It holds just a few fish, mostly cutthroat and a few rainbow, all big and extremely shy. On a good day I might hook one or two of these and leave several flies hanging from the surrounding snags. Yet a nineteen-inch cutthroat captured from such water, admired briefly and then carefully returned, is a memory ever to be savored.

Of course the Pacific Northwest has no monopoly on beaver ponds. They can be found wherever there is cold, running water, lots of trees and a population of eager beaver. I imagine they all offer similar fishing. But beaver ponds have not fared well in the face of metastasizing suburbs; many have been drained, bulldozed, filled in or artificially landscaped to provide centerpieces for tasteless "developments." Others, yet beyond the reach of subdivisions, have been spoiled by logging. So there aren't as many beaver ponds as there used to be.

Nevertheless, there are still some good ones left—dark little jewels of water hidden back in the woods, filled with dark little jewels of trout. If you make the effort to find them and fish them, I promise you won't be disappointed.

Well, not every time anyway.

RESCUE MISSION

O ne year it was the middle of July before I had a chance to fish the North Fork of the Stillaguamish. The river looked the same as always, but I soon found subtle changes left by the winter floods; some pools were deeper, others had filled in, and the places where summer steelhead would hold were all a little different.

But one thing had changed hardly at all: The old flood channel back in the woods still ran as straight as an arrow, a tunnel through the canopy of maples and alders that grew on either side of it and kept it in nearly perpetual shade. I had found the channel a couple of years earlier and discovered it offered a perfect shortcut to the downstream pools I most liked to fish. It cut squarely across the base of a long peninsula formed by a great oxbow bend in the river, saving at least a quarter-mile hike.

The only human footprints I ever saw there were my own. Not that there weren't other tracks—those of many deer, several rac-coons, an otter or two, once even the tracks of a solitary cougar. I gladly shared the hidden channel with them, but as far as other fishermen were concerned, it was as if I had my own private trail to the downstream pools.

That day in July I came to a place in the channel where some past flood had dug a hole around the base of a root, and the hole was filled with what I supposed was rainwater. It was scarcely more than a puddle, maybe four feet long and half as wide, with no more than six inches of water in its deepest part. Soon it would surely dry up in the summer heat, which penetrated even here beneath the shade.

I had nearly passed it by when I saw a flash of movement in the pool and stopped to take a closer look. To my amazement, the tiny pool was filled with trout and salmon fry, at least forty or fifty of them, darting about in confusion. Some were a good three inches long, and it was obvious they had been trapped in the pool for a long time—probably since the last big freshet filled the channel back in April. That they had survived so long in the summer heat and found enough food to stay alive was truly remarkable.

But it was obvious they weren't going anywhere. The pool was at least several hundred yards from the river, and when it dried up— as it surely would—they would all die.

Many young salmon and steelhead die this way, in drying potholes far from the main channel of their native river. Nature tries to account for this by assuring there are always enough young fish so at least a few will survive, no matter how many are lost. That worked well enough before humans began interfering with watersheds and rivers, doing all the nasty things we've done to them. Now the wild salmon and steelhead in this river, as in so many others, are in danger of extinction, so the fry trapped in this lonely little pool had enormous value. It seemed tragic to think that even one of them might die.

I left the pool and went on about my fishing, but stopped on the way back and again studied the fish trapped in the little pothole. Watching them, considering their plight, and admiring their hopeless struggle for life, I decided to try to help them. Next day, when I came back this way, I would bring something I could use to catch at least a few of the trapped fish, then carry them to the river and release them.

A small dip net would have been ideal for the purpose, but of course I had none. A look around camp produced nothing better than an empty margarine container to use as a net and a plastic bag I could fill with water and use to carry the fish to the river. Thus equipped, I set out next morning for the little pool hidden in the woods.

When I got there I filled the plastic bag with water, then took the margarine container and started trying to scoop up fish. I had known it wouldn't be easy, but it turned out to be even more difficult than I'd supposed. The fry were remarkably quick and perfectly camouflaged, their finely spotted backs blending invisibly with the rubble on the bottom. Not only that, but a big white margarine container is hardly the best thing to use for catching wary, fast-moving fingerlings.

After fifteen or twenty frustrating minutes, during which I caught exactly nothing, I decided to build a dam across one end of the pothole and leave a narrow opening in the middle. Then I'd try to herd the fish through the opening and block it with the margarine container so I could trap them when they tried to swim out again. I built the dam with rocks, then waded into the pool to drive the fish through the opening. It almost seemed as if they knew what I was trying to do; not a single fish went through, and soon I had stirred up so much silt that I could no longer see the fish at all.

In the end, after more than half an hour of trying, I managed to catch only a single fish. It was about three inches long, heavily spotted and healthy looking. At that size it's hard to tell a salmon from a trout, but based on the shape of its fins and its overall appearance, I judged it was a tiny coho. I was disappointed I had been unable to catch any of its companions, but one fish was better than none, so I dumped the fingerling into the plastic bag full of water and started for the river.

At the end of the flood channel, where it opens out onto the river's main stem, there is a patch of tall grass and tangled blackberry that effectively hides the channel's entrance from anyone passing by. The blackberries, though, are a hazard to waders, so I was watching my feet carefully as I pushed my way through the tangle, not paying much attention to the plastic bag full of water in my hand. Suddenly I felt the bag brush against a blackberry vine; water immediately began spouting from four or five holes.

Forgetting my waders, I dashed the rest of the way to the river, holding the leaking bag in front of me. There was still a little water left in it when I got to the river's edge, and I quickly knelt in the shallows, opened the bag, and poured out the remaining water.

The coho—if that's what it was—waited until the very last second, then shot out of the bag into the river, darted into the current, and vanished from view.

I wondered where its journeys would take it, and hoped it would range far across the North Pacific, growing all the way, and eventually return as a bright, strong adult, perhaps to this very spot, and sow the seeds of many others of its kind.

The odds against many fish being able to do that are long indeed. But at least now they were one small fish better than before.

HOW NOW BROWN TROUT

It doesn't fight as well as the rainbow, it's not as pretty as a brook trout and it's far more particular in its habits than the pragmatic cutthroat. So what makes the brown trout, *Salmo trutta*, so special?

The main thing is its reputation for being the smartest of all trout. That's not to say brown trout are mental giants; their brains are no larger than those of any other trout, about the size of a pea. They really aren't any smarter, either; brown trout have just learned to be more cautious and wary, and therefore somewhat harder for fishermen to catch, than other trout species.

The brown trout occupies a lower rung on the evolutionary ladder than either the rainbow or cutthroat, so its survival skills theoretically shouldn't be any better than theirs, if as good. So how did it get to be more cautious and wary than they are? The answer is that the brown trout has a much longer history of association with people.

Those were brown trout rising to the first flies dapped by the Macedonian fly fishers whose exploits caught the eye of Aelian, the Italian-born naturalist who wrote in Greek, and thus found their way into what is generally acknowledged to be the world's first written description of fly fishing. But Macedonians and others were undoubtedly fishing for brown trout even before Aelian's time and they've had plenty of company ever since.

So what happened? The dumbest brown trout were the first to be caught by the Macedonians and their fellow anglers, and thus were removed from the gene pool. Through many succeeding generations, human fishermen unwittingly continued subjecting the brown trout to a sort of selective breeding program, removing more and more dull-witted trout from the population while leaving their sharp-witted cohorts to reproduce. The result, over time, was a more wary breed of trout, one adapted to survive not only in the wild but also to cope with the predatory tactics of human anglers.

Which is why the modern brown trout enjoys a reputation for being tough to catch: It's the product of centuries of angling mortality that removed all but the quickest and best trout from the gene pool. It has been bred selectively for survival, and its reputation for being smarter than the average trout has won the respect of anglers wherever browns have been introduced around the world.

The brown trout might enjoy even more respect in this country if it weren't an interloper. Browns are not native to North America, although like many other immigrants they have made themselves at home here, especially in the eastern United States. In those waters, browns have often crowded out the native eastern brook trout, much to the chagrin of some anglers.

Browns are less common in the West, especially the Pacific Northwest, but that merely gives them a little extra local cachet—like Coors beer used to have when you couldn't buy it in Washington or Oregon.

The term *brown trout* was rarely heard when I started fly fishing; instead, people called them Loch Levens or German browns. Both strains had been introduced locally and although they were basically the same fish, they looked different, with dissimilar colors and spot patterns—probably relics of having come originally from different European environments.

The Loch Levens were by far the more handsome of the two, at least in my view. With creamy yellow flanks and dime-sized red and black spots, they were so colorful they might have inspired some of the tartans for which their native Scotland is known. The German browns, by contrast, tended to be dark and dour, with less prominent spots.

Both varieties were usually stocked in company with another species, mainly rainbow trout. Few local waters, if any, were inhabited exclusively by brown trout, a situation that continued many years.

Then, in the early 1970s, fly fishers started whispering the secret that Quail Lake, a small body of water near the town of Othello in eastern Washington, had been stocked only with browns. I went there to see if the rumors were true, found out they were, and went back many times. It wasn't because the browns were such great fighters—they weren't, although they sometimes ran well and nearly always put up a dogged struggle—but just because they were such a novelty.

I also confirmed the truth of something else I'd heard and read about them: They were far more active at night than during daylight hours, perhaps another result of centuries' worth of angling mortality having culled all the daylight feeders from the gene pool. Sometimes, when I visited Quail Lake in the daytime, the fishing was so dead I'd have thought the lake barren had I not known otherwise. But if I returned after dark, there were almost always trout feeding—you could hear them rise, even if you couldn't see them—and I caught many by casting a fly blindly into the darkness.

The first year I fished there I noted the curious fact that the trout were all about the same size, fifteen or sixteen inches in length and about a pound and a half in weight. That made me think the lake had been stocked only once. The next year, when I went back, the trout hadn't grown any—they were all still about the same size and weight—and that made me begin to suspect something was wrong. Such proved to be the case: Sunfish had gotten into Quail Lake and were eating everything in sight, leaving little food for the browns.

One more year and it was all over. The lake eventually had to be poisoned to remove the rapidly growing sunfish population. When it was restocked, the state decided to put in rainbows instead of browns, so that was the end of Quail Lake as a brown trout fishery.

Dry Falls Lake, a spectacular body of water that was once the scene of a mammoth prehistoric waterfall, is another venue where it's possible to catch brown trout. But rainbow trout constitute the bulk of the lake's population, so it's always something of a surprise when a brown takes your fly.

That wasn't always true. In past years, when the lake's water level was higher than today (a leaky dam has kept the lake well below historical levels for the past decade), there were spots where you could almost be assured of catching a brown trout. Once you learned the location of these places—and there was nothing about their appearance to distinguish them from any other place—you could return with a high degree of certainty that if you put your fly in the right spot, a brown trout would be waiting to take it. That predictability lent a certain charm to the fishing; if you grew tired of catching rainbows, you could always go find a brown trout or two, and chances were good they'd be larger than any of the rainbows you'd caught.

They were also very pretty. I don't know the source of the brown trout stocked in Dry Falls Lake, but their new home evidently agreed with them. They were nearly always healthy, positively glowing with color, and they had spots the size and color of ripe raspberries and blackberries.

Those surefire brown trout spots disappeared after the lake's water level began to fall, and I haven't yet learned where the new spots are—if there are any. I still catch an occasional brown trout in Dry Falls, but not nearly as many as before.

Current thinking in fisheries management is that it's a bad idea to continue stocking "exotic" species; better instead to let indigenous species occupy the available habitat. Since the brown trout is an "exotic" species—meaning it's not from around here—that could mean its days as a sport fish in the Northwest are numbered.

That would be a shame. The brown trout has won the affections of many Pacific Northwest anglers, including mine. It adds a touch of variety to the lineup of species that gives spice to an angling life. If it disappears from the Northwest scene, you can be certain there will be many who will mourn its passing.

EARLY AND LATE

I've never especially enjoyed getting up early in the morning and there are only a few things I consider important enough to make me do so. One of them is summer steelhead. Or at least that used to be the case.

Morning and evening are the best times to fish for summer steelhead. Of the two, morning is better; the fish are bold then, scattered around the river even in the shallow places where you will never find them in the brighter light of day. They've had a whole long night to forget about all the flies and lures they saw the day before, so a fisherman has a clean slate to start with. The water hasn't yet been disturbed by wading anglers wearing noisy metal-cleated brogues or by successive waves of kayakers, canoeists and inner tubers. There's no doubt that the first light of morning, when the river still is streaked with mist, the dew is yet wet upon the leaves and the birds are still busy with their morning songs, is the very best time of all to go fishing for summer steelhead.

The trouble is, everybody knows that. I'm usually not in a very good mood when I get up early—rather like an old grizzly awakened prematurely from hibernation, I suppose—and it does my disposition no good at all to rise well before dawn, rinse the sleep from my eyes, fumble into my waders, grope my way through the dark woods down to the river—and then find half a dozen anglers standing in line ahead of me. And that has happened enough times over the years that I don't do it anymore.

Instead, I now sleep in, rise late, enjoy a leisurely breakfast and stroll down to the river around nine or nine-thirty or sometimes even later. By then the early rising anglers have all disappeared, gone back to bed I suppose, or perhaps retired to grumble and sulk about being crowded out of their favorite riffles. It's still too early for the people in kayaks, canoes and inner tubes, so for a while I will have the river all to myself.

It's true that by then the bloom is off the rose—the water has been disturbed, the fish are wary and alert, and maybe some already have been caught—but it's a lot better than getting up at an ungodly hour only to get stuck in the piscatorial equivalent of a supermarket checkout line.

When I start fishing late I try to imagine what those early morning fishermen would have done and then do something different, try to give the fish a look at a fresh fly or at least a different method of presentation. Sometimes it works and sometimes it doesn't, but when a fish does respond my sense of satisfaction is even greater than it would be otherwise. After all, by nine-thirty in the morning, the steelhead are all on guard, and if you succeed in catching one anyway—well, that seems like more of an accomplishment than if you had taken one by surprise in the dawn's early light.

I fish in the evening, too. So does everyone else. Evenings are good because the fading light seems to prime the steelheads' curiosity and get them restless and moving. They roll more often then than at

any other time of day, and it's easy to see them and mark their positions so you can cast to them. This is exciting because there is always greater anticipation when you *know* you are fishing over fish than when you are merely fishing the water, without knowing whether any fish are there. I guess that's the main thing that keeps me fishing in the evening, because I hate crowded rivers—even when most of the people in the crowd are my friends.

Usually I fish until it's too dark to see what I'm doing. But I've fished the same places long enough that I can wade the river safely and find my way back to camp even in complete darkness—something I wouldn't try to do if I didn't know the water.

If I catch a fish in the evening, that's good. If I don't, then to hell with it; I'll go back to camp, have dinner, smoke a cigar, read a book and go to bed late so I can sleep in the next morning.

Somehow, when I fish the evening, I don't feel I have as much invested in the effort as I did when I used to get up before dawn; rising early always seemed an unnatural act, a form of cruel and unusual punishment. Evening fishing is easier; you can slide in or out of it without much thought or effort. It seems to come naturally and feel right.

Best of all, you don't have to get up early.

SHAD OCCASION

My fly rod, reel, waders and a box of shad flies were in the trunk of the rental car and I could practically feel them urging me onward as I drove across the Virginia countryside. Glancing at the road map lying open on the seat, I could see it wasn't much farther to my destination.

I'd fished for shad before—in California's Yuba and American Rivers and on the Washington side of the Columbia River below Bonneville Dam—but this was different. This required a much longer road trip than any of those waters, and there was more to it than just fishing. This was also a journey into history.

I was headed for the Nottoway River. I'd be first to admit that in terms of fly-fishing destinations, the Nottoway River doesn't rank anywhere close to the Yuba, the American, the Columbia or just about any other river you'd care to name. In fact, it might not be on anybody's list but mine. Chances are you've never even heard of it, and there's little reason you should—except that this otherwise unremarkable little stream played a role in a pivotal event in American history.

It happened in early spring, 1865. Robert E. Lee's tattered, half-starved Army of Northern Virginia was drawn up in a thin crescent south and east of Petersburg, pressed on every side by the more numerous forces of Ulysses S. Grant. In late March, Grant dispatched troops under General Phil Sheridan to try to turn the Confederate right flank.

Lee had no choice but to respond, so he thinned his own lines even more and sent several brigades under General George Pickett to counter Sheridan's move (yes, that was the same Pickett who gained immortality for his gallant, doomed charge at Gettysburg).

At first Pickett did well, pushing a Union cavalry force back toward the hamlet of Dinwiddie Court House. But then his men brought in two prisoners from the Union V Corps, an ominous sign; if the veteran V Corps was in the neighborhood, it meant Pickett was outnumbered and his troops were in an exposed position. He decided to retreat and assume a defensive posture.

So on the morning of April 1, Pickett's weary troops began plodding back over the muddy route of the previous day's advance. Federal forces snapped at their heels but did not press them. Hunger was a greater problem than the enemy; some Rebel artillerymen, desperate for rations, stole corn from their horses' feed bags.

Late in the morning Pickett's ragged column reached the road junction known as Five Forks. There a message from Lee was waiting: "Hold Five Forks at all hazards." The critical junction was the key to Lee's right flank.

Pickett posted his men in earthworks running east and west from the junction and sat back to await developments. As the day wore on, the front grew quiet. The tired, wet, hungry Confederates took advantage of the respite and settled down to rest.

For cavalry general Tom Rosser, the lull offered a chance to do something he had been anticipating eagerly. Several days earlier,

Rosser and his men had been on the Nottoway River a few miles southwest. Shad had been running in the Nottoway, and the young general had caught many with a borrowed seine. He still had some in his headquarters wagon, and after the privations of the past few days the mouthwatering thought of baked shad was very much on his mind.

Rosser found a spot near Hatcher's Run, about a mile north of Five Forks, and arranged for the fish to be cut in half and placed on sticks propped next to a fire. He dutifully sent invitations to his superior officers, Pickett and General Fitzhugh Lee, to join the feast. Both officers were probably just as hungry as their men and accepted the invitation gladly.

Everything remained quiet at the front, so at the appointed hour the two generals headed for Rosser's camp, neglecting to tell anyone where they were going.

The shad bake was a very pleasant affair: good comrades relaxing around a warm fire, exchanging lively conversation and eating a hearty meal. Surely a flask was handed back and forth and cigars were lit in accompaniment. It was peaceful there by the muddy little stream in the scrub pine thickets, warm next to the coals where the fish had been baked, and the war seemed very far away. Hours passed and nothing was heard from the front—no distant thump of artillery or roll of musketry.

Then, close at hand, came a sudden spatter of rifle fire. The startled generals looked up from their fire to see a line of blue-clad soldiers emerging from the woods. Pickett leaped to his feet, called for his mount and galloped toward the front. Union troops fired, but Pickett got past them somehow and dashed for Five Forks. He had not gone far before he was engulfed by a panic-stricken mob of fleeing Rebel troops—the remnants of his command, streaming away from the front.

While the generals had been stuffing themselves with shad, Sheridan had launched an overwhelming attack. An atmospheric quirk had kept the sounds of battle from being heard in Rosser's camp, and by the time the three generals learned what had happened it was far too late. Without their generals to lead them, Pickett's force had been routed and the whole Confederate line was unhinged. Petersburg and Richmond would fall within hours and Lee's army would be forced to begin its final march. Eight days later Lee would surrender at Appomattox.

All that happened more than 135 years ago, but shad still run in the Nottoway River every spring. It seemed to me that catching one would provide a sort of living link to the past, making the history of those long-ago events come alive as nothing else possibly could. So I planned a visit to coincide with the date when Tom Rosser caught his shad in the Nottoway, figuring the run should then be at its peak.

But my first stop was the lonely spot on Hatcher's Run where the three generals gathered for their shad bake. It seemed as peaceful as it must have been before the Yankee soldiers appeared suddenly on that spring afternoon so many years ago. From Hatcher's Run I drove to Five Forks, where Confederate earthworks are still visible, then headed southwest toward the thin blue line on the map labeled NOTTOWAY.

Passing through villages with names that still echo in the history books, I came finally to my destination, a muddy little streak of water flowing through dense, vine-tangled woods. The river was impossibly high after heavy spring rains, spilling over its banks in places, its color matching the blood-red soil of Virginia. You've heard the old saw about rivers too thick to drink but too thin to plow; the Nottoway, on this occasion, was nearer the plowing than the drinking stage. I could see at once that if any shad were hidden in its rusty flow, there was no chance of taking them on flies. No wonder Tom Rosser had used a seine.

So I left my tackle in the trunk and just sat and watched the river for a while, contemplating how its fish had changed the course of history. And I couldn't help wondering: Would the Civil War have ended differently if not for those few shad? What might have happened if Pickett hadn't liked shad because of all the bones?

Or suppose Tom Rosser had believed in catch-and-release?

MONDAY NIGHT SALMON

Sometimes, when the score on *Monday Night Football* gets a little out of hand, Al Adams turns off the game and watches the salmon instead.

You could do that, too, if you lived in a home with a salmon stream running through the living room. Adams designed and built such a home on the western shore of Mercer Island in Lake Washington, just east of Seattle. The house was designed with twin foundations separated by a ten-foot gap to accommodate a stream. Electric pumps were installed to draw water from Lake Washington, supplying about a hundred gallons a minute to the stream.

When Adams, his wife, Edee, and their four children moved into the house in 1970, all they had in mind was "a pond, running water and maybe some trout." There were no fish until February 1974 when a friend offered Adams about three hundred coho salmon fry left over from an experiment at the University of Washington. Adams put the fish in his stream where they stayed until they had grown to smolt (migratory) size. Then they left to begin a journey through the lake to its outlet to Puget Sound and beyond.

Watching the little salmon grow into smolts got Adams thinking about a long-term salmon-rearing project. Biologists checked his backyard stream and told him it was well suited for rearing coho salmon. Enlisting the cooperation of a marine biology class at nearby Mercer Island High School, Adams got a state permit and went to work. He and several students from the class went to a state salmon hatchery and spawned four female and three male adult coho salmon.

The spawning yielded about twelve thousand fertilized eggs, which were placed in a redwood trough built by Mike Erickson, one of the students. The trough was set up amid the plants in Adams' greenhouse and water siphoned from the artificial stream was allowed to flow through the incubating eggs.

When Christmas came in 1975 Adams got a special present: the hatching of the first tiny fish. "It excited me no end," Adams says. Within the next three days, nearly all the eggs that were going to hatch did so—about ten thousand of the original twelve.

When the tiny fish—known at that stage as alevins—were ready to begin feeding, Adams transferred them to a pond next to the greenhouse. Thanks to frequent feeding with commercial fish food, the salmon were ready by summer to begin their long journey to the rich pastures of the Pacific.

Once in salt water, coho salmon spend about eighteen months feeding and growing until they reach sexual maturity, then return to their river of origin with almost unerring instinct. But birds, other fish, marine mammals and commercial and sportfishermen take a heavy toll along the way, leaving perhaps only a single adult survivor from every hundred smolts that went to sea.

If any of the three hundred salmon released into Adams' stream in 1974 survived to adulthood, they should have returned in the fall of 1976. Not surprisingly, none did. But there were greater hopes for the ten thousand fish hatched in his greenhouse; the adults from that group were due home in the fall of 1978.

On October 19, 1978, Adams found a bright four-pound adult coho salmon in his stream. The fish was dead, although there were no visible signs of illness or injury.

"That really tugged at me a lot," Adams says. "I hesitated quite a bit to accept the fact that it was one of our fish." The cause of its death was never determined.

But within the next few days other adult salmon began to make their way up his tiny stream, and Adams knew his fish were finally coming home. "Then I relaxed and started to enjoy the trip," he remembers. In all, 140 salmon returned to his stream that year.

After that adult salmon began congregating off the mouth of Adams' little stream in late October of each year. Then, one by one, they made their way up a seven-step fish ladder leading through Adams' living room to the backyard pond below the greenhouse where they'd first known life. The spectacle of their return was visible through a glass enclosure inside Adams' house, and it was something his family never grew tired of watching.

There were some anxious moments, however. Most were due to power failures that stopped the pump supplying water to Adams' little hatchery; without running water, eggs or newly hatched alevins

will die quickly from lack of oxygen. Adams responded to these crises by organizing family bucket brigades to keep water circulating through the hatchery.

One violent storm left the power off at Adams' home for more than twelve hours. Al and Edee grew sore packing water buckets to the hatchery, but the egg crop survived.

The original redwood hatchery trough was expanded with the addition of fiberglass trays, giving the hatchery a capacity of one hundred thousand eggs. Adams' state permit allowed him to release only thirty thousand fish a year, however, so any surplus salmon were loaded aboard state hatchery trucks and taken elsewhere for release. A fish pathologist examined the salmon before each release to make sure they were healthy.

Adams, a salmon fisherman, began to "evolve a different frame of mind" about fishing after he started raising his own. He wasn't worried about catching one of his own fish—chances of that were infinitesimally small—but he found himself "getting more and more into the mind-set of catch-and-release. I get a real pleasure out of catching a beautiful fish, looking at it and then letting it go."

Adams sold the Mercer Island home in 1986 and moved to a new residence near the small town of Union on the south shore of Hood Canal, a giant saltwater fjord that skirts the eastern shore of the Olympic Peninsula. Missing the annual return of his home-reared salmon, he soon enlisted the help of a sixth-grade class from the Hood Canal School and started raising chinook and fall chum salmon in a small natural stream flowing into Hood Canal next to his new home. The natural stream doesn't flow through his living room, but Adams can still see it through a glass door—and he was watching when the first adult chinook and fall-run chum salmon began returning to spawn.

This went on for several years until Hood Canal summer-run chum salmon were listed under the Endangered Species Act, prompting state authorities and local Indian tribes to put the clamps on fish-rearing projects that might pose competition for the endangered summer chum. That included Adams' efforts to raise chinook and fall-run chum salmon.

So Adams was out of the fish-rearing business, but that didn't keep him from pursuing his passion for salmon in other ways. He began working with the state department of fisheries and wildlife, the Hood Canal Salmon Enhancement Group and the Mary E. Theler Organization, which owns and operates the Theler Community Center and Wetlands in the town of Belfair at the "toe" of Hood Canal. Their common objective: Establish a Pacific Northwest Salmon Center on a twenty-five-acre site next to the Theler Wetlands.

Plans call for the center to include a thirty-two-thousand-square-foot building with enclosed artificial salmon-spawning stream, theater, interpretive center, computer and research laboratories, aquarium, library and offices. The 220-foot artificial spawning stream will be enclosed in glass so visitors can observe every aspect of salmon spawning behavior, even the development and hatching of eggs buried in the gravel. A nearby natural stream also will be restored to provide spawning habitat.

An anonymous donor kicked in fifty thousand dollars to pay for the design. As this was written, efforts were under way to raise twelve million dollars to purchase the site and pay for construction, and another six million to provide an endowment fund for operations and maintenance. The mission of the center will be to preserve wild salmon runs—not just those native to Hood Canal waters, but all species.

As an officer of the nonprofit corporation spearheading the venture, Adams is deeply involved in the fund-raising program. He also has found another way to express his ever-growing admiration and respect for salmon. A couple of decades ago he began making wood carvings of salmon, using old-growth western red cedar as a medium.

He has sold several pieces as artworks and one, called *The Dance*, was chosen as the logo for the Pacific Northwest Salmon Center.

Now seventy-four and retired from his dental practice, Adams says he spends most of his time bringing salmon to life in wood and rarely fishes anymore—"maybe twice in the last fifteen years." But he still has fond memories of the return of that first coho salmon to his little Mercer Island stream. "The shot of passion or adrenaline when that first little coho returned is what got me started on all this," he says.

The home on Mercer Island has changed hands three times since he sold it, but the first two sets of owners kept the artificial stream and its hatchery going. Adams isn't sure if the current owners are continuing the tradition.

Yet he doesn't worry about it, either. Now his attention is focused on another stream, and this time he doesn't have to worry about power failures. The little creek flowing into Hood Canal next to his new home carries about three times as much water as the Mercer Island artificial stream, and the water comes from natural sources that won't dry up if the power fails. And although he no longer is involved in raising them, chum salmon continue to return to the stream every fall. Adams has counted as many as three hundred chum returning to spawn, though he says the stream is so small that only about twenty adult fish can fit into it at a time.

When they do, and the score on *Monday Night Football* gets a little out of hand, Al Adams can still turn off the game and watch the salmon instead.

FEBRUARY

Give me a bright cold February day when the rivers are as low and clear as they will ever be in winter. Give me that and a willing steelhead ready to rush my fly and I will ask for nothing more.

Usually there are such days in early February, a succession of bright spots in the otherwise dreary winter, received gratefully after December's torrential rains and January's relentless gloom. For several days or more the skies are clear and pale blue and the winter sun, low on the horizon, glints and flashes from the great gleaming snowfields of the Olympics and the Cascades. The nights are brittle cold and shot with bright stars and ribbons of aurora, the days scarcely above freezing, and down in the great wide valleys the rivers drop back into their channels in a translucent green flow different in color from any other season of the year.

By then the steelhead runs are well along, with most of the fish having come in from the sea during the higher water of the preceding months. By then they have been back long enough to renew acquaintance with the rivers they last knew as smolts before starting their long journey to the sea. But things are different now; the returning fish seem almost too large for some of the rivers that have drawn them back, and the narrow pools and riffles are impossibly confining after the limitless reaches of the ocean. So the fish are restless and wary as they wait in the cold clear flow until the eggs or milt are ripe within them.

These February days are wonderful for fishing. Stripped of their summer foliage, alders and cottonwoods stand along the riverbanks in naked brown silhouettes braced against the pale blue winter sky. Beyond them are ranks of fir and spruce and cedar that so far have escaped the loggers' saws; they look thicker and greener in winter, as if each were clad in its own heavy overcoat. Fantastic fringes of moss and lichen grow on damp cedar shakes or old rail fences, each a tangled little mysterious colony of life that looks like a tiny fairy-tale forest when you view it closely.

Wood smoke blooms from the cabin chimneys, rising straight into the windless sky, and the sweet scent of burning alder floats pungently in the still winter air. Deer browse brazenly in the open, knowing they have the forests and fields to themselves this time of year. The paths leading down to the rivers are lined with last fall's crop of dead leaves, now decaying into mold, and all the puddles are rimmed with ice. Snow lies in frozen patches back in the shade of the woods, looking like scattered crusts of old stale bread. The cold, clean air seems to enhance every human sense so that each sight, each sound, each scent and feeling is somehow more intense, more vivid, more keenly experienced than at any other time of year.

The river flings back the reflection of the sky, and the sound of its passage seems muted in the hush of winter. It curls whitely around the boulders that stand stubbornly in its path, dashes briskly through the riffles, swells and wrinkles through the deep passages, backtracks in confusion through the eddies. The river is blind, forced to search by feel for its outlet to the sea.

The water, when you enter it, seems so cold it hurts, even through insulated waders. The bright fly is like a spark rising from a campfire as it travels swiftly through the air and falls softly to the translucent current, then pauses in response to a long mend of line. The rhythm of fishing is familiar and comfortable, and the exertions of wading and casting help keep the cold at bay, at least for a while.

Even at low water, a winter river seems less willing than a summer river to disclose its secrets. Part of it is the river's color, that peculiar winter-green flow unique to the season, always promising much but revealing little; part of it is the light, always pale and diffuse, coming from a sun reluctant to leave the horizon, never rising far enough to cast its illuminating rays into the river's depths. So a winter angler, like a winter river, must search mostly by feel.

He must also have patience and stamina for the long haul, enough to keep going all through the day, from the cold gray dawn to the frosty dusk, enough never to lose hope that a fish may yet be found somewhere in the unfathomable green depths of the river.

The strike, when and if it comes, is a strong, slow pull, growing ever stronger, perhaps with a knuckle of water on the surface to mark the place where the fish has turned. The fish itself is a bar of silver in the pale green flow, then a bolt of lightning as it throws itself into the air in a shower of sun-filled water droplets. Then it runs with wild strength back toward the sea from whence it came, turns in response to the restraining force, and jumps again. This goes on until at last its strength is spent and it lies in exhausted submission where you have eased it up gently on a sloping gravel bar. There you see for the first time how truly beautiful it is: a gleaming sculpture of gunmetal, nickel and chrome, with speed and strength built into every graceful line, a perfect gift from the sea.

Such fish do not come often on these bright, memorable February days; just often enough to keep an angler's hopes alive. But even fishless days hold the high reward of experience on the stream, and the chance to test every human sense to its very limit. Surely there is no better place to spend a day than on a river, and no better time than February.

YESTERDAY'S MAGIC

Yesterday was perfect. I could do no wrong. Every cast was on target, I had chosen exactly the right fly, the fish all were big and strong and no matter what they did I landed every one of them.

It's true the day didn't start that way; in fact it began very unpromisingly. But the perfect part—that's the part I remember. That's the part I'll always remember.

I was on a Columbia Basin desert pond, a sprawling, weedy, trout-rich water exactly like a chalk stream except it lacks current. On still, glassy days when the sun is bright it can be an exceptionally difficult water to fish; the trout are shy and the conditions allow them to inspect your offerings at their leisure, which they do, and if they find the slightest fault with either your fly or your presentation, you will be utterly rejected.

But yesterday was not like that. The weather was cool and dark with a threat of rain. When I started fishing in the morning the hatch had not yet begun. Rises were few and far between. It did not look like an auspicious day for fishing.

The pond holds a wide variety of insects, all desirable and available to trout, but the most numerous—and most avidly sought by trout—is the chironomid. The chironomid is more commonly known as a midge, which may be an appropriate name for the smaller species usually found on eastern rivers and lakes, but is something of a misnomer in parts of the West. On this particular pond a "midge" may be as minuscule as its standard eastern counterpart or as large as a small grasshopper—big enough to tempt even large trout to rise. Chironomids come in many different colors and hatch almost every day of the year. Several different sizes and colors may hatch in a single day, sometimes all at once, and it can be difficult to figure out which color and size is the trout's preferred choice.

Yesterday's hatch began in late morning with smaller insects, perhaps the equivalent of a size 14 or 16 fly pattern, and they were almost turquoise in color. As soon as the first flies appeared on the surface, big trout began rising to take them with explosive, heavy sounds. In my fly box I found a pattern that came close to matching the size of the adult, but not the color. So I looked instead for an imitation of the pupa and found one that matched the color but not the size. I settled for the latter, hoping the trout, in their eagerness to feed, would overlook the fact that my imitation was too large.

One trout did. I covered a large, violent rise and the fly was seized instantly by a big rainbow that darted away on a blistering run. It took all the fly line and a considerable portion of backing from the reel before it finally stopped, and for the next few moments I reeled frantically, trying to recover most of what the trout had taken. After that we traded line back and forth until the trout finally tired of the contest and I coaxed it in. It was a fine, bright rainbow, close to three pounds. I twisted the barbless fly free and let it go. Confident now, I resumed casting with the same fly, but no other fish came near it. The hatch waxed and waned; one moment it seemed there were flies and rises everywhere; the next there were only a few flies and scattered rises. And none of the rises was to my fly.

Then it started raining—a mild drizzle at first, then big wet drops and lots of them. I struggled into the bulky rain gear I had brought and resumed fishing.

The hatch seemed to taper off in the rain. It tapered off even more when the wind began blowing, stirring a riffle and driving the raindrops hard against my back. It grew colder. Four hours passed and I failed to take another fish. The weather, if anything, was growing worse.

But that's the part I scarcely remember now, because it was all eclipsed by what happened next.

It started in midafternoon. Despite the weather, another hatch of chironomids began, and this time I found in my fly box a floating pattern that seemed a close match in size (12) and color (yellow) for the natural. The trout quickly validated my judgment.

Over the next two hours, until the hatch ended, it seemed I was hooking and fighting big fish constantly. They took the fly with spectacular splashing rises and flashed away on that characteristic long first run. Five different fish ran out long lengths of backing; several others ran shorter distances but jumped repeatedly. One ran far into the backing and then took both line and leader into a dense thicket of weeds; I slacked off and waited until the trout found its way out again. The line and leader miraculously followed, free of snags, and I recovered all the line and backing and landed the trout. Another fish took the line around a clump of tules, but I threw a long loop over the waving stems and the line fell clear in open water on the far side; I got that fish, too.

It seemed I hooked every fish that rose within casting range, then managed to outwit it at every violent turn. While other anglers fishing nearby were catching little or nothing, I could do no wrong. I felt their

envious glances and sensed their frustration. It was just my day; I had
the right fly and the right touch, and nothing could go wrong.

In those furious two hours I released fourteen trout from seven-
teen to twenty-one inches. When the hatch finally died out and the rise
stopped, I was dead tired and ready to quit. But I was happy, too, and
felt like maybe I was just about the very best trout fisherman on earth.

But that was yesterday.

Today I went out on the same pond, confidently expecting to
repeat yesterday's magic. Today the sky was clear, the sun bright and
the wind even stronger than it had been the day before. There was
only a sparse hatch and the flies were a different size and color than
the ones I'd seen yesterday.

I fished the same places where I had done so well yesterday and
caught nothing. Another angler, fishing nearby, hooked fish after fish
and played them through long runs from a screaming reel. He guided
them skillfully away from the weeds, lowered his rod to their jumps
and landed every single one. All of them were big. With other nearby
anglers, I looked on enviously and muttered in frustration.

Yesterday had been my day; today belonged to someone else.
Tomorrow it probably would be another angler's turn.

But I'll always remember yesterday's magic. And maybe, if I'm
lucky, one day soon my turn will come again.

Part Five

THE STATE OF THE ART

Tackle is not meant to be an end unto itself, though it is an easy cultural fallacy to believe otherwise.

—HARMON HENKIN, *FLY TACKLE,* 1976

I say every so often, like a preacher who feels that he hasn't made a point in his sermon if he's said it fewer than nine times, that in this kind of fishing the fish is much less important than the act, or the art, if you will, of fishing.

—ARNOLD GINGRICH,

THE WELL-TEMPERED ANGLER, 1965

Take Me to Your Leader

I started fishing back in the days when gut leaders were the only kind available, which gives you some idea how old I am. Gut had to be soaked in water or glycerin the night before you went fishing or it would be as stiff and brittle as broom straw. Even while you were fishing you had to keep spare leaders moist to preserve their pliability. At the end of the day you had to dry them out to keep them from rotting. It was a lot of fuss and bother.

Synthetic leaders liberated us from all that, but the first ones had many problems. Often they were as limp as warmed-over spaghetti. Many of them stretched, kinked, coiled or refused to hold knots. Their advertised breaking strength frequently was off by several decimal places. A trout would swim by, stop and look, and the tippet would break.

All that was a long time ago, but it's hard to tell whether we've made much progress since then. One thing, however, is certain: Today's vastly increased fishing pressure, the growing popularity of catch-and-release, and the resulting numbers of leader-shy trout have made it more important than ever to have a strong, fine leader with a nearly invisible tippet.

Believe it. Trout may not read the same books or magazines you do, but they aren't so feeble-minded that after being caught two or three times it doesn't occur to them that the sight of a leader attached to a fly might mean another nasty trip to the trout's equivalent of an oral surgeon. So fine leaders, especially tippets, are vital for angling success.

I became convinced of this when I began to notice that the brand of nylon tippet material I had used successfully for many years just wasn't getting the job done anymore. For a while I stuck with it anyway—brand loyalty is a powerful thing, and I liked the way the material held knots and turned over flies—but finally, after watching many educated trout shy away from my all-too-visible tippet, I realized it was time to start searching for something else.

So I began experimenting with leader material from a wide variety of manufacturers, both foreign and domestic. Some, I discovered, had better memories than I do. I'd tie on a fly and suddenly the leader would remember that in a former lifetime it had been part of the coil springs on a pickup truck, and behave accordingly.

Others proved as spineless as the average politician, incapable of turning over even a size 14 dry fly. Still others turned out to be as slippery as liquid soap. I'd tie two sections together with a blood knot, tug gently on the ends to snug the knot tight, and—presto!—it would slip out.

(By the way, in case you've ever wondered how the blood knot got its name, I have two theories: One is that you're usually sweating blood by the time you finally get the damn knot tied, the other is that—since the knot requires using both hands—you can't swat mosquitoes while you're tying it, and consequently they are free to draw blood.)

I also found that breaking strength remains a great mystery, even with state-of-the-art leader materials. About the only thing you can be sure of is that the breaking strength is *not* what's advertised on the package. It may be more, it may be less. It may vary with temperature or the age of the material, or—for all I know—with the Dow Jones average.

Here's a rule of thumb: The breaking strength of leader material will always be *more* than advertised when your fly is hung up on an underwater snag or an overhead branch and you're trying purposely to break it off. In those circumstances, the tippet will always hold and the leader will break halfway up. Conversely, the breaking strength will always be *less* than advertised when you're playing a fish. Under those circumstances, a ten-inch trout can break a tippet rated at 6-pound test.

Despite many frustrations, I kept experimenting, and at long last, after excruciating trial and error, I found a brand of tippet material that doesn't coil like a bedspring, is capable of turning the fly over, and sometimes even holds knots. Most important, the trout can't see it.

The trouble is, I can't see it, either. Even under a bright sun on a still day, wearing my new bifocals, I can barely make out the stuff. I'm forced to tie knots mostly by feel, which takes a lot longer, and sometimes I don't get them right. But when the knots hold, the stuff really works.

Except for one other little problem: Like every other leader material I've ever used, this stuff floats. I know, because even though I can't see the tippet itself, I can see its shadow on the bottom.

This is not surprising. Leader material is the best floating substance known to humankind. If it were used to make life jackets, it would probably save thousands of lives a year. Short of adding lead—which I refuse to do, because I think then you're getting into shot-putting instead of fly fishing—there seems no way to sink the stuff.

I'm certain of this because I've tried everything, including all the old-fashioned nostrums of toothpaste, shampoo, mud, carbon tetra-chloride, fuller's earth and various other homemade and commercial concoctions. Nothing works. Even the thinnest, otherwise almost in-visible tippet lies there merrily on the surface, casting a shadow about as subtle as the trans-Alaska pipeline. Trout gather to rest in the shade.

You'd think a society capable of sending men to the moon could make leader tippets that sink. But we haven't done it yet.

Even if we do someday, there are other challenges to be met. How about leaders that are resistant to wind knots? (I had a wind knot once, so I know what a problem they can be.) Or how about droppers that don't tangle?

Things to hope for, perhaps, but I doubt I'll live long enough to see them. Meanwhile, if you'll pardon a little doggerel, this is my leader refrain:

THE BALLAD OF THE TANGLED TIPPET

Orvis and Umpqua and Mason and Ande
Platyl and Gladyl and Stren;

Maxima, Aeon, Cortland and Climax
I've used them all now and then

Some slip, some slide, some are brittle and break
Some are as limp as a length of spaghetti

Some remember, some don't, some won't do anything but
Twist like a strand of confetti

Some crinkle and wrinkle and form tight little ringlets
That refuse resolutely to sink

These twisted, tangled, tormenting tippets
Will haunt me forever, I think.

THE ARCANE ART

The Friday-evening dinner conversation at Corbett Lake Country Inn was all about fids, nodes, splines and Japanese water stones. An outsider might have thought himself at a convention of crossword-puzzle enthusiasts, but it was really just a gathering of devotees of the once almost lost art of building bamboo fly rods.

About forty builders from six states and two Canadian provinces had come to this pastoral lodge in the hills near Merritt, British Columbia, for a weekend of demonstrations, debates, fishing stories and an opportunity to try out one another's bamboo rods.

Not so very long ago such a gathering would have been impossible. As every ardent fly fisher knows, bamboo rods once reigned supreme among fly anglers the world over, but that was before fiberglass, graphite and boron came along. Even as those new space-age rod materials were catching on, the raw material for bamboo rods—Tonkin cane (*Arundinaria amabilis*, literally "lovely bamboo")—was growing more and more difficult to obtain. Tonkin cane grows only in a small area of southeast China, and exports had been virtually nil since the Japanese invasion of China before World War II. By the 1950s, prewar cane stocks built up by American commercial rod builders were beginning to run out. The outlook for bamboo rods was gloomy. Only a few commercial builders continued to offer them, and the ranks of amateur builders were reduced to a stubborn few.

Then two events, little noticed at the time, breathed new life into the art of cane rod building. One was the 1972 Nixon administration rapprochement with China, which led to at least a fitful resumption of trade in Tonkin cane. A more powerful catalyst was the 1977 publication of *A Master's Guide to Building a Bamboo Fly Rod* by Everett Garrison and Hoagy B. Carmichael, a remarkable book that revealed many secrets of the rod maker's art and started a quiet rod-building renaissance in basement workshops all over North America.

John Bokstrom of Maple Ridge, BC, and Don Andersen of Rocky Mountain House, Alberta, were among those caught up in this quiet revolution. They became friends and hatched the idea for the first bamboo rod builders' conclave.

Corbett Lake Country Inn was a natural choice for such a gathering because its proprietor and French-trained master chef, Peter McVey, also is a noted bamboo fly-rod builder. The question was who else to invite; Bokstrom and Andersen knew only seven other amateur builders. That problem was solved by issuing a general invitation through a fly-fishing magazine. The invitation drew twenty-six rod makers to the first conclave at Corbett Lake in the spring of 1988. The meeting was judged such a success that another was held two years later and another two years after that.

I have worked with cane enough to understand its powerful attractions, but in no sense am I a qualified bamboo rod builder. So it came as a pleasant surprise when the mail brought an invitation to attend one of these conclaves, even though I knew it would be more as observer than participant.

The gathering opened with the Friday-night dinner, then resumed next morning with an intense six-hour session interrupted by only a single fifteen-minute break. Bokstrom moderated and the rod makers—all men, although a few patient wives also sat in—collectively examined each step in the process of building a bamboo fly rod.

What followed was a conversation you could not have heard anywhere else. There was talk about the continuing uncertainty of Tonkin cane supplies, about the best way to split culms (lengths of cane still in the round) and a lively debate over preferred methods for straightening nodes, the knotty stem joints of the bamboo.

Jeff Walker, a commercial builder for the R. L. Winston Rod Co., said he used a hot plate and teakettle to steam the nodes until the bamboo fibers became pliable enough to straighten by hand. Another builder said he preferred "a heat gun with 475 watts out the nozzle." Others argued that open flame is best.

Bokstrom said less heat is required if the cane is soaked in water first. "I got that idea from Peter McVey, who leaves his cane out in the rain," he said.

McVey demurred. "I spit on it," he joked.

After nodes are straightened, the planing process begins. Metal planes are used to cut the individual bamboo strips, or splines, that are later glued together to form rod sections (most builders at the conclave followed the conventional six-strip construction method, but adherents of four- and five-strip construction also were represented). Mild controversy ensued over the relative merits of Japanese water stones and Arkansas stones for sharpening plane blades.

More friendly sparks flew over the esoteric question of blade angles. Some builders said they prefer less than thirty degrees, others thirty to thirty-five, while some said they used forty or more. One told of a friend who had made a planing form by laminating pieces of old hockey sticks.

More debate followed over the virtues of various glues. Bob Milward, a rod-building architect from Vancouver, BC, said he prefers G-2 epoxy for several reasons, among them the fact that "you don't even have to refrigerate it, so you never end up with funny mayonnaise."

Someone said it's a good idea to apply alcohol to the cane before adding glue. "Even a good Scotch will do," he said.

After gluing, splines must be bound tightly under pressure while the glue sets. Ray Gould and John Byrd of Edmonds, Washington, demonstrated the use of a fid—a tapered tool for separating braided fibers—to insert glued-up rod sections inside a piece of polypropylene rope. Then they stretched the rope on a device resembling a medieval torture rack so that as the tension increased, the braided strands closed around the glued-up rod section, binding the splines tightly together.

Ferrules are added after the glue has cured. Good ferrules always have been difficult to obtain, and some builders told how they make their own. Then the conversation turned to cork, traditionally used for rod grips. Portugal always has been the source of the best cork, but the rod makers complained that quality is declining swiftly. Some blamed the wine industry for using too much of the available supply, but that didn't stop them from draining a considerable portion of McVey's wine cellar over the weekend.

The session finally broke up late Saturday afternoon. Some rod builders headed for the bar to continue debate while others went outside and took turns casting one another's rods in a gusty spring breeze.

Discussions resumed as soon as the breakfast dishes were cleared away next morning. This time the topics were rod tapers, computer programs for designing rods and calculating stress curves and a planing demonstration that left part of the dining-room carpet buried under bamboo shavings. Then, after final handshakes and farewells, the rod makers went their separate ways, their heads brimming with new information and ideas.

If the weekend proved one thing, it's that bamboo rod makers don't agree on very much of anything. As one put it: "There's been some damn good bamboo fishing rods made by every method." So there's no "right" way to build a bamboo fly rod—just a lot of different ways.

But it also proved something else: A lot of people are trying those different ways, and the arcane art of building cane fly rods— once nearly lost—is alive and well again.

Coping with Technology

Fly-fishing technology is changing so fast these days it's hard to keep up. I'd barely figured out what "Swannundaze" is, let alone how to pronounce it, when a host of new synthetic fly-tying materials with equally exotic names hit the market. I was still trying to grasp the concept of "modulus" in graphite rods when Sage came out with something called "sixty-four million modulus," not to mention a "Durascrim" finishing process. G. Loomis, meanwhile, began touting a nonglare "stealth" finish on its rods.

Now I feel more confused and out of date than ever.

It's not that I'm old-fashioned, mind you. Or, on second thought, maybe it *is* that I'm old-fashioned. It's true I started fishing back in the days when people were still using gut leaders, silk lines and bamboo rods—mainly because that's all they had to use.

The gut leaders had to be soaked overnight in water to soften them up, then carried in tins lined with moistened felt through the day's fishing. The silk fly lines required a lot of attention, too; they had to be stretched before you used them and dressed frequently to keep from getting waterlogged. The bamboo rods were great, but they were heavy by modern standards, and a long day of fishing could put a real strain on your wrist.

Today, if you had to soak your leaders before using them, dress your fly lines often or cast with a heavy rod, you'd think it was a real pain in the backcast. But I don't remember we ever thought of such things as a bother; bamboo, gut and silk were state of the art back then. That was just the way things were.

Advances in technology have changed all that, and now just about every aspect of fly fishing is easier and more comfortable—and somehow more complicated. The changes are coming so thick and fast it's all getting to be a great big blur, and I wonder if it's ever going to stop—or if it's all necessary.

One thing that would make it easier to understand and keep up is if all the advertising copywriters and marketing gurus would back off and stop trying to think up clever, high-tech names for new products and processes. Consider:

Fly-Rite Extra Fine Poly Dubbing Material, Cyclops Eyes, V-Rib, Krystal Flash, Hare-Tron, Lura-Flash, Flashabou, Liqui-Lace, Microweb wing material, Chinese boar synthetic bristle, Microfibetts, ceramic scissors, scissors with ice-tempered blades and a whole bunch of other new stuff for fly tying.

Titanium frames, Teflon and metal disc drags, polyurethane epoxy coatings, Delrin gears and lots of other new gimmicks for fly reels.

New fly lines with maximum "bubble load," "graduated densities" and "migrating lubricants," not to mention Kevlar Super Loops for attaching lines to leaders.

Waders made of polyurethane-coated Supplex, or trilaminate fabric with a nylon tricot lining, or "an ensolite foot bottom to eliminate compression leakage;" inflatable suspenders with "200 denier oxford nylon [and] urethane coated inflation chambers" and fishing shirts made with "hydrophobic" mesh that "transports ('wicks') moisture away from the skin, enhancing the body's natural 'evaporative' cooling process."

Let's see—isn't "maximum bubble load" something you get from drinking too much champagne?

If you lost a rod with a "stealth" finish, could you ever find it again?

"Migrating lubricants"—does that mean they drip?

Does anybody really know what all this stuff means?

Help!

The other day I was thumbing through a mail-order catalog and ran across this sentence describing a new rod case: "The rod is stored in a lined and baffled polyurethane tube, which is covered with 1000 denier Cordura." The tube isn't the only one who's baffled.

Here's another: "Up until now polypropylene has been the most functional underwear available, but Capilene is superior in every way." And here I am, still wearing cotton.

While thinking about all this, and trying to figure out how to cope with it, I was suddenly inspired (if that's the right word) to pen the following, which might not be very profound but somehow made me feel better anyway. I offer it with no apologies to advertising copywriters:

ENOUGH, ALREADY

New fly-fishing products in profusion
Have caused me nothing but confusion;

Till now the postman's daily tread
Fills me with a sense of dread.

For I know another catalog'll
Just add more to my mind-boggle!

Each day, it seems, there's something new
From Liqui-Lace to Flashabou;

New suspenders that inflate;
Line densities that graduate;

Waders only microns thick;
Shirts that really are a wick;

Dubbing made of propylene;
And underwear of Capilene!

Lura-Flash, migrating lubes,
Super Loops and baffled tubes;

Ceramic scissors, Cyclops Eyes,
Synthetic bristles for your flies;

Stealth rods, V-Rib, ensolite,
Hare-Tron, Delrin and Fly-Rite.

Enough, already! So I say,
Give me back the good old days

Of silk and gut and rods of cane;
No Teflon and no urethane.

It's all so different now, I fear,
You have to be an engineer

To understand these high-tech terms;
Either that, or fish with worms.

"OLD YELLER"

I t's the ugliest fly rod I own. The shaft is sooty gray and the windings a dismal shade of yellow—the only color of rod-winding silk
I happened to have at the time—and the whole thing is spattered
with frozen droplets of epoxy from my clumsy efforts to refinish it
each time I've replaced worn-out guides. From an aesthetic stand-
point it leaves almost everything to be desired . . . and yet in its own
way this beat-up old graphite rod represents a small piece of fly-
fishing history.

I used bamboo rods when I started fly fishing because that's all
there was. Later, when fiberglass rods came along, I joined the rest of
the world and started using them. They were cheap, strong, lighter in
weight than bamboo and apparently the answer to every fly fisher's
prayers. Fiberglass rods had just one problem: Their tips vibrated after
each cast, throwing waves in the fly line. Nevertheless, most anglers,
including me, were willing to overlook that flaw in exchange for the
many benefits of fiberglass. I acquired a whole stable of fiberglass rods
and fished hardly anything else for more than a decade.

Then I started hearing rumors about a new miracle rod-making material called graphite, supposedly even stronger and lighter than fiberglass. With graphite rods you were supposed to be able to cast farther; what's more, graphite was rumored to solve the vibration problem. When you cast a graphite rod, the tip supposedly stopped still, allowing line to shoot forward straight and true.

The rumors remained just that—rumors—until Jim Green, rod designer for the Fenwick Company, called one February day and invited Alan Pratt and me to visit the Fenwick manufacturing plant on Bainbridge Island in Puget Sound and try casting some of their first graphite rods. The rods weren't finished, Jim explained; in fact, he hadn't even decided what models to include in the company's forthcoming product line. As a former world-champion caster, he recognized the need for input from a couple of ordinary casting mortals, like Al and me, before making any final decisions. He was familiar with our casting styles from our earlier collaboration on a book about fly casting and thought we'd make good guinea pigs for his new rods.

Wet snow was falling when we drove off the ferry and headed for the Fenwick plant. Jim greeted us in his usual soft-spoken manner and led us outside to a parking lot with many deep, water-filled potholes, some apparently large enough to hold trout. Snowflakes the size of chicken feathers were spiraling down and dissolving as they hit the puddles. Jim carried a fistful of prototype graphite rod sections and joined them together one by one, then handed them to us and stood back to watch as we tried casting.

Each rod was fitted with a reel seat and cork grip, but the guides had been mounted only temporarily, held in place by Scotch tape. After we had cast each rod a number of times, Jim asked what we thought of it, and if we suggested the rod didn't feel quite right—if it seemed a little top-heavy, or if the butt and tip sections didn't seem quite fully synchronized—he would take the rod inside and make a few quick alterations, perhaps trimming a bit from the tip section, or respacing the guides. Then he would bring it back outside and ask us to try it again.

I had always thought rod design involved plenty of deep thought and lots of complex mathematical equations, and maybe that's true early in the process. But at this stage Jim used a seat-of-the-pants approach: If something didn't work the first time, then trim a little here, shave a little there, move the guides around and try again. And that's what we did until, after Jim's careful and repeated tweaking, each rod began to feel comfortable in our hands.

We also quickly verified the rumor that graphite solved the vibration problem. The tip of each rod stopped dead after each cast and the line shot straight and true to its target. That alone was reason to inspire enthusiasm for the new material.

The wet snow had turned to rain and we were soaked and chilled by the time Jim was satisfied we had given his test models a fair trial, and as we prepared to leave he offered us each a rod in thanks for our help. I opted for a seven-and-a-half-foot rod for a 6-weight line, a combination I like for fishing dry flies on lakes. From the meager supply of graphite rod blanks Fenwick had so far produced, Jim found a pair of butt sections and a single tip and gave them to me. "Try these and see which butt section works better," he said.

All the sections were dark gray, almost black, resembling the lead in a No. 2 pencil—not surprising, since they were made of essentially the same stuff. I took them home, attached a ferrule and guides to the tip section—using that miserable yellow winding silk— and mounted reel seats, grips and guides on both butt sections. Then I took them outside and tried casting.

It was obvious one of the butt sections simply wouldn't do. It was so much stiffer than the tip that the difference in action almost created a hinge effect in the middle of the rod, causing the line to flop around in large, awkward loops.

But the other butt section worked in perfect rhythm with the tip, the two making music together, and the resulting casts were long, straight and true—with no hint of after-vibration. I coated both sections with varnish, set them aside to dry, then went out and got a cloth bag and an aluminum tube in which to keep my first graphite rod.

That was more than thirty years ago. That little graphite rod has seen a lot of action since. It has flexed under the weight of countless trout and salmon and was the rod I used to catch my first sea-run cutthroat on a dry fly in salt water, perhaps the first cutthroat ever caught by that method in the salt.

The rod has been bounced around in boats speeding over rough water, put away wet, and several times narrowly escaped destruction from slamming car doors. In fact, it has endured many indignities to which a good fly rod should never be exposed, but it's still just as serviceable as the first day I used it.

Perhaps I'd take better care of it if weren't so ugly. It's still the same sooty gray color and still has those same miserable yellow windings, which is why I've taken to calling it "Old Yeller." Jim and Al are both gone now, so the rod is my only tangible reminder of that long-ago day we cast those first Fenwick graphites in the Bainbridge Island

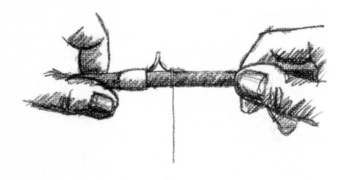

parking lot. That in turn reminds me that Old Yeller is one of the very first graphite fly rods ever made.

I suppose that qualifies it as something of an artifact of fly-fishing history, and that's a good reason I should take better care of it—even if it is too homely ever to think of displaying in a museum.

Maybe I'll start doing that one of these days. Meanwhile, I think Old Yeller and I still have a few more fish to catch.

THE COMPLEAT FLY TYER

I won't mention the full name of my friend, John W., the fly tyer. It might embarrass him and I would not want to do that.

John, you see, is one of those generous souls who ties flies and gives all of them away. Psychiatrists might find him an interesting case because he would rather give away flies than do anything else. A strange affliction, but a welcome one as far as his friends are concerned because John does tie beautiful flies.

One day a mutual acquaintance advised me that John had given him a new pattern, which he had used with unusually good results. "You ought to get over to John's place and get him to tie you a few," my acquaintance said.

I took his advice and at first opportunity drove to John's house in the suburbs. I opened the front gate and a dozen barred rock roosters ran out between my legs.

I knocked and John's wife opened the front door about an inch. She peered through the narrow opening and recognized me from prior visits. "He's around back," she said, and closed the door.

I walked around the house, flushing a condor as I did so. The great bird flew up into a tree, where it startled a flying squirrel.

John was in the backyard, skinning a gazelle.

"Hi, John," I said. "Where did you get the gazelle?"

"The zoo," John said. "Zookeeper said the poor thing died of old age." He looked around carefully to be sure nobody else was listening. "The truth is, I slipped the critter a good shot of rat poison. Gazelle fur makes wonderful nymphs."

I thought he was kidding, but you never can tell about John.

"I hear you've got a hot new fly pattern," I said.

"Yeah," John said as a snowy owl landed on his shoulder. He shooed the bird away. "I'll tie you a bunch. Great new pattern."

I wandered around his backyard while I waited for him to finish skinning the gazelle. There was a big birdbath in one corner where a peacock, a scarlet ibis and a Reeves pheasant were competing noisily for a bath. A blue Andalusian rooster fluttered underfoot, pursued by an arctic fox. A muffled roar in the hedge turned out to be a polar bear cub. John's backyard is one of the most interesting places I know.

Soon John finished skinning the gazelle and led me inside. He sat down at his fly-tying bench, illuminated by a bank of huge strobe lights. It was surprisingly cool under the lights. Then I saw the new air-conditioning unit that controlled both temperature and humidity.

John noticed me eyeing the air conditioner. "Did you know that jungle cock begins to deteriorate at a temperature of eighty-nine degrees and a humidity of ninety-eight percent?" he asked. "That air conditioner cost me nearly a thousand bucks, but it sure has saved a lot of jungle cock. It dissipates the heat from my hook forge, too."

"What's the new fly pattern?" I asked.

"I'm glad you asked. It's a combination of spun wombat fur and the urine-stained fuzz from a female kangaroo. The body is ribbed with titanium tinsel and then I top off the whole thing with a couple of turns of albatross hackle."

"Sounds good," I said.

"Yeah, this is one of my best yet," John said. His skilled, nimble fingers were almost a blur as he fashioned the delicate fly. He paid no attention to the groundhog curled up under his chair.

Within a few minutes John pressed half a dozen exquisitely dressed flies into my hand. I started to thank him, but he brushed it aside.

"As long as you're here I'll tie you a few drys," he said. "I've got a new one—trumpeter swan quill body mixed with alpaca fur, wings of passenger pigeon breast and hackle from a Siberian snipe. I've got a rhinoceros coming next week and I'm trying to figure out how I can work that in."

I shooed two porcupines and a rabbit out of a chair and sat down. A water buffalo peeked through the window and winked at me. In a few minutes John handed me half a dozen beautifully tied dry flies. "There. Try those," he said.

I thanked him and rose to depart. Then a last thought occurred. "By the way, John, are these flies good for rainbows or browns?" I asked.

"How the hell should I know?" John said. "I've never caught a fish in my life. Can't stand the slimy things." He kicked a giraffe that had been leaning against him and I went home.

SILVER BULLETS AND EXPLODING FLOATANTS

One day when it was raining too hard to go fishing I decided to run an Internet search for the term *fly fishing* and see what happened. What happened was that I got more than six million hits.

Of course it's unlikely all those hits had to do exactly with fly fishing. Considering the vagaries of Internet search engines, some of them probably were about fly swatters or ice fishing or almost any other subject with the word *fly* or *fishing* in its name (a similar search on the word *flies* turned up Web sites featuring "men's fly-front underwear," Venus flytrap plants and several other wholly unexpected topics).

On the other hand, most of those six million hits probably *were* about fly fishing in one form or another, and the astounding number is evidence of the Internet's enormous influence on the sport.

Much of that influence has been positive. The Internet is surely the most convenient method yet devised to shop for fly-fishing tackle. Nearly all the traditional mail-order catalog houses—Orvis, L.L.

Bean, Hook & Hackle and many others—now have Web sites with online ordering, and there are many new enterprises that sell only on the Internet. The Internet also offers the chance to find great tackle bargains through online auction services such as eBay.

Other Web sites, such as abebooks.com, make it possible to locate and purchase just about any fly-fishing book published within the past century, sometimes at cut-rate prices. Countless fishing camps and lodges also have sites that provide trip-planning information and allow anglers to book reservations online. Once you've done that you can go to other sites that promise the lowest airfares, make your reservation and order your e-ticket.

Such services are a great boon to fly fishers, but the Internet offers another great advantage: You can use it to find out just about anything you want to know about fly fishing. Those interested in the history of the sport can check out a Web site called flyfishing history.com, the work of Dr. Andrew N. Herd, MD, a physician, editor of *Waterlog Magazine* and member of the Flyfishers Club of London. His site offers biographies of prominent anglers and articles on such esoteric subjects as how to refinish old silk fly lines. The emphasis is on British and European fly fishing, but that's to be expected since the sport originally developed in Britain and Europe. Unlike many Web sites, this one also has nothing to sell except a couple of books, and the sales pitch for those is remarkably low-key. There's even a brief, humorous autobiography of Dr. Herd.

History buffs also can check out amff.com, the Web site of the American Museum of Fly Fishing in Manchester, Vermont (although an in-person visit to the museum is much more satisfying).

Several Web sites offer the online equivalent of fly-fishing magazines, complete with classified ads, features, bulletin boards, river-flow information and links to fishing organizations. Dates and locations of fly-fishing shows around the country also can be found online by visiting flyfishingshow.com. There you will even discover lists of exhibitors and "celebrities" scheduled to appear at each show.

Some sites post articles or features and ask readers to rate them or file responses. Sometimes these responses can be brutally frank. One site I visited asked readers to rate its articles for both interest and usefulness; one disgruntled respondent said an article "put me to sleep" and rated its usefulness as comparable to "a screen door on a submarine."

Not all fly-fishing sites are free. Some are "clubs" you must pay a fee to join, with varying services offered in return. Others are free to visit but offer plenty of high-priced stuff for sale. One such, foolafish.com, advertises a "spray-on formula" that "takes advantage of the new Scientific Discovery that fish hunt for food and prey by using a fourth color totally invisible to humans." Maybe "foolafisherman.com" would be a more appropriate name.

Ease of communication is another great advantage of the Internet. Through "chat rooms," "bulletin boards" or "discussion forums," anglers can stay in touch with their counterparts all over the world, exchanging information, sharing fishing reports or even inviting Internet pen pals to go fishing with them. Most users of these sites refrain from using their real names, however; instead they identify themselves by using fishing-oriented, lowercase pseudonyms, such as "weightforward," "sinktip," "eightweight," "wetfly," "troutcrazy" and so forth.

It's possible to spend a great deal of time perusing these bulletin boards and discussion forums, but much of that time will inevitably turn out to be wasted. That's because most sites are unmonitored and lack standards of any kind; as a result, they are often little more than electronic sumps of mediocre thought and verbiage, cluttered with stream-of-consciousness fishing reports, rumors, speculation, profanity, miserable grammar and atrocious spelling. But those who search patiently and persistently may occasionally find a nugget of genuinely useful information or real humor.

Or sometimes something just downright strange. One fly fisher posted a bulletin-board message asking if anyone could recommend a good recipe for homemade liquid fly floatant. Another angler responded with a formula calling for white gas, "Triclorethaine," and paraffin, a highly explosive mixture that was supposed to be boiled on a stove. The recipe concluded with this warning: "Do not make this stuff, the manufacture of this stuff can be hazardous to your health . . . serious injury or death can result in trying to make this stuff."

Several bulletin boards recently displayed a newspaper article about a serious incident of "river rage." The article described a confrontation on Utah's Green River in which a wading angler got into a beef with a boat fisherman. Things escalated until the boat fisherman drew a pistol, whereupon the wading angler retreated quickly and put in a call to the local sheriff.

Sheriff's deputies tracked down the man with the pistol, who turned out to have a concealed-weapons permit. He also denied the gun was loaded or that he'd ever pointed it at the other angler. Deputies referred the matter to the local prosecuting attorney for follow-up action.

The unspoken message to anglers: Be careful.

Another bulletin board carried a sad but unfortunately not uncommon message from an angler who reported he had tried to buy a fly rod over the Internet, but after sending his money to the seller he never heard another word—a frequent hazard of Internet shopping.

Same message: Be careful.

One day I received an e-mail from a friend who forwarded an item he had found posted on a fly-fishing bulletin board, one he thought would be of particular interest to me. It was a report from an angler who had just visited a popular local fly-fishing lake where he had met another fisherman who impressed him deeply:

> This guy's cast was one of the best I've ever seen. He was
> throwing 60-plus feet of line with a 26-foot leader like it was

nothing. A 26-foot leader!!??!! Around 3 P.M. this guy is getting his [boat] loaded up when he comes over to us to show us something, a bunch of stuff he pumped out of a fish's belly. We start talking, and it's obvious this guy has been around, seen some things. Really nice guy, he gave us a B.C. lake gem [British Columbia fly pattern].

After we chatted for a bit, he busts out some fly boxes. His boxes were like nothing I've ever seen. Nothing from a shop, all custom, every last one. We chat some more, he takes off. As soon as he leaves, it hits me.

That was Steve Raymond!

We all just looked at each other. . . . So I honestly don't know, I guess I'll never know. But some of the things he said were just amazing. If this guy wasn't writing books about fly fishing, he should have been. A total professional fly fisherman in every sense of the word.

Hmmm. I'm afraid the angler was mistaken; whoever this super-flyfisher was, it wasn't yours truly. I've never used a twenty-six-foot leader in my life, and I wouldn't ever want to be mistaken for a "professional fly fisherman," whatever that is.

Besides, I always leave a silver bullet.

(Just kidding.)

The Internet unquestionably will continue to have a huge impact on fly fishing, as it has had on nearly everything else, and it's difficult to imagine what the next few years may hold. Perhaps "virtual reality" fly fishing will turn out to be the wave of the future, and the next generation of anglers will do most of their fishing on the Internet.

Far-fetched? Maybe not. Recently I came across a Web site offering "a full 3D, physics-based fly-fishing game featuring accurate fly-casting dynamics, multiple destinations, different types of fish, and realistic fish behavior." With the game you could "practice overhead casting, roll casting, mending, dry and nymph fishing, and other fly-fishing techniques." Not only that, but "if you catch the biggest fish, you will get your name on our trophy page." The site offered a free demonstration copy, or the full version could be purchased for "only $24.95."

I didn't order the game, but the description reminded me of something the late, great Sparse Grey Hackle once wisely said: "You don't learn fishing from a book; you learn it from a fish."

You don't learn fishing from games or the Internet, either. You still have to learn it from a fish. And that's how it always will be.

So turn off your computer and go fishing.

THE SOUND OF SILENCE

When I was coming of age as a fly fisher I was advised by various old-timers that just about any reel would do as long as it was a Hardy. The venerable Hardy reel, made in England, was highly regarded for its rugged construction and reliability, but mostly it was admired for the fabulous Churchillian sound it made when a fish was taking line from its spool. Whether by accident or design, the engineers who fashioned the clicks on Hardy reels had discovered a frequency that seemed to resonate up and down the human angler's spine. It was an exuberant sound, a delicious sound, one that added a full extra measure of tingling excitement to every struggle with a heavy fish.

And it was infernally loud. There was no need to whoop or holler when you tied in to a good trout; the Hardy would do the talking for you. You didn't even have to steal a glance to know that every other angler within a quarter of a mile was looking your way, doubtlessly feeling envious and perhaps admiring your skill for having hooked such a good fish.

Hardys also could be useful in other ways. I remember once hiking into a remote desert pond rumored to hold sizable trout, and when I stood on the shore and pulled the first few lengths of line from my Hardy LRH, a cluster of mallard ducks immediately began quacking in response. That was when I realized that if you pulled line off the reel in just the right increments at just the right speed, the Hardy LRH could do double duty as a serviceable duck call.

That was the Hardy for you. No matter where you fished, you could hear its happy sound. In those days the Hardy was to fly fishing as the Harley is now to motorcycles.

Whatever happened to that joyful noise? I suppose Hardys still make it, although the new ones have become so expensive I can't afford to find out. But now the market is flooded with dozens of other fly reels designed to meet every conceivable fishing situation, from tiny trout in small brooks to mighty marlin on the high seas. These reels are triumphs of modern technology. They are light in weight but still so rugged you could probably run over one in a truck without hurting it. Some have drag systems stout enough to slow down the space shuttle. They're available in traditional gunmetal finishes or metal-flecked psychedelic colors, and I suppose it won't be long until you'll be able to buy tie-dyed reels.

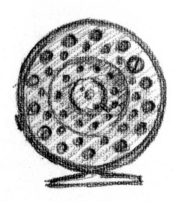

The only trouble is, hardly any of them make any noise. When a fish runs, about the most you can hope for is a sound like that made by a well-fed kitten. You could play a bonefish in the reading room of the public library without disturbing anyone.

I first noticed this unfortunate trend some years ago when my friend Dave Draheim purchased a new reel from a well-known manufacturer. It was a handsome thing with a flashy gold finish and it looked mighty impressive when he clamped it on the reel seat of his fly rod and went fishing. But the first time he hooked a big fish that started taking line from his reel, there was . . . nothing. Dave tried to fill the vacuum by creating his own sound effects, but we both agreed they fell short of the reel thing (pun intended).

A few years ago I was playing a bonefish at Christmas Island when the drag system of my reel (not a Hardy) failed suddenly. The reel started free-spooling and line shot in all directions. Then the reel seized up, allowing the fish to pop the leader and escape. I took the smoking reel apart and saw immediately that its insides had been scrambled beyond repair. Fortunately I had a backup with me: an old Hardy St. John. I put it on and resumed fishing. Soon I hooked another bonefish, a good one, and the St. John announced it to everyone within earshot—which included just about everyone on the island. Other anglers, some far distant, turned their heads. "Geez, what a racket!" I heard one say. Frightened by the sound, hundreds of frigate birds, terns and boobies lifted off their island perches and circled overhead, squawking and flapping. I loved it.

But the St. John wasn't made for hard use in salt water, so after the trip I went looking for a new reel to replace the one that had exploded. Every one I tried was silent, or nearly so. Why is this? Do the reel manufacturers think we want to keep it a secret when we've got a good fish on? Have they forgotten that magical extra dimension a screaming reel adds to a battle with a memorable fish? It makes you wonder if these guys ever go fishing themselves.

I've heard it said that the only legitimate reason for a reel to have a click is so a guide can tell when a fish is taking line, since the guide might not be able to see the reel from his vantage point. In my opinion that's not the only legitimate reason, but even if it were, the clicks on many new fly reels aren't loud enough for a guide to hear even if he's leaning over your shoulder, or wearing a hearing aid. Some reels don't have clicks at all.

My late friend Alan Pratt was another noisy-reel aficionado who also had a rare talent for crafting ingenious inventions and devices. Together we once conspired to create a reel with a phonograph record or compact disc on its inside plate so when a fish began taking line the reel would begin playing Schubert's *Trout Quintet*. The saltwater version would have featured the theme from the television series *Victory at Sea*. Of course we never got around to doing it, but I now offer the idea free of charge to any reel manufacturer bold enough to try it. Just imagine: a tie-dyed reel in psychedelic colors that plays music when a fish takes line.

Maybe you think that sounds crazy, but in my estimation just about anything would be better than the wimpy whispers or absolute silences that emanate from most of the new fly reels on the market.

Or am I the only one who feels this way? Frankly I doubt it, and to show support for a return to noisy reels I'm thinking of having some bumper stickers printed. They'd say: REEL FLY FISHERS HAVE LOUD CLICKS.

Let me know if you want one for your bumper.

A MATTER OF DEFINITION

The stream curled swiftly around scattered boulders and spilled
into deep, mysterious pockets. Trout were holding well down in
the pockets, watching and waiting for the current to bring them food.
An angler was fishing for them, using a nymph with a pair of split
shot pinched on his leader, lobbing short lengths of line upstream and
counting on the extra weight of the split shot to sink his fly down to
the level of the waiting trout.

Undeniably effective. But is this really fly fishing?

Salmon were spawning in the river and a fresh run of steelhead
had followed them upstream. Loose eggs from the spawning salmon
drifted downstream in the current, and now and then a steelhead
would see one coming and move to take it. A clever angler, knowing
this, was fishing for the steelhead, casting a long sinking line with a
small bright fly tied to resemble a drifting salmon egg.

Undeniably effective. But is this really fly fishing?

A fisherman stood on the marshy shore of an alpine lake,
watching as trout bulged occasionally in the open water. He was

armed with a spinning rod and a monofilament line with a bobber at the end; attached to the bobber was a short leader with a small nymph knotted to the end. The fisherman cast the bobber far out into the path of the bulging trout and let it settle on the surface, with the fly dangling underneath. Then he sat back to wait for a fish to come along and take it.

Undeniably effective. But is this really fly fishing?

It's true that in each of these cases the anglers were using something called a "fly." But is a "fly" tied to imitate a salmon egg really a fly? And even if an angler uses a realistic imitation of an insect, can he truly be said to be fly fishing if he uses a spinning outfit and a bobber to present his imitation to the fish? And what about the angler with weight on his leader? When a fisherman adds so many split shot that casting becomes more like the shot put, is he really fly fishing in the traditional sense?

These are difficult questions. What makes them difficult is that even now, centuries after the sport of fly fishing was invented, we still have no commonly accepted definition of what it is.

It's not that there has never been any attempt to arrive at such a definition; throughout the long history of angling literature a number of writers have addressed the problem. Most notable of these was the late Frederic Halford, who established the doctrine that the only proper method of fly fishing was to cast a dry fly upstream to an individual rising fish. Halford's effort was memorable because he came closer than anyone else to making his definition stick; his pronouncements, echoed by friends and supporters, made the upstream dry fly the only socially acceptable method of fly fishing in late nineteenth-century England. After a while it took on the aura of holy writ, as if it had been engraved by lightning on stone tablets carried down by Halford from a mountaintop. Any other kind of fly fishing was considered boorish behavior, even sinful, and anyone who practiced it risked becoming an outcast from the angling fraternity.

But even Halford's rigid purism didn't last very long. G. E. M. Skues soon demonstrated the legitimacy of the nymph as a rival method, and in the New World it wasn't long before Gordon, LaBranche and others showed there were many alternative ways to fish the dry fly with no apparent danger of corrupting one's soul in the process.

Human nature being what it is, it was inevitable that Halford's rigid dogmatism would be challenged and overturned. That this happened was not only natural but healthy, for no human activity—fly fishing perhaps least of all—can grow and mature if its followers lack the freedom to experiment with new concepts and ideas.

Even so, there have been other attempts since Halford's time to define or codify fly fishing. All have been unsuccessful and most have been attended by controversy. Some years ago I unwittingly found myself squarely in the middle of one such controversy.

It began when the Federation of Fly Fishers decided to draft a model fly-fishing regulation and submit it to all the states and Canadian provinces in the hope that many would adopt it. Eventually, it was thought, this would lead to common regulations throughout all of North America, so that no matter where you fished, you could always be sure the rules were the same.

It seemed like a good idea at the time, and much to my surprise and consternation, the federation's president appointed me chairman of a committee of anglers whose task was to draft the language of the model regulation. The committee even had an attorney to make certain its definition was legally sound.

The committee spent several months doing research, including a careful reading of the fly-fishing regulations that already had been adopted by many states and provinces. The most promising ideas were sifted from these and compiled in a list that was intended to be a starting point for further discussion.

The list was circulated among the federation leadership—not as a proposal, for we were still a long way from that, but merely as a status report on the committee's work. Nevertheless, it set off an immediate furor, and angry letters quickly started pouring in. All had a common theme: Do as you please about everything else, but if you so much as even think of trying to draft a regulation prohibiting the use of (a) double hooks, (b) metal-core lines, (c) chumming, (d) weighted flies or leaders, or (e) practically anything else, then the letter writer promised to (a) resign from the federation, (b) persuade all his friends to do likewise, (c) start a rival organization, (d) punch everybody on the regulations committee in the nose or (e) carry out any of a great number of other imaginative threats.

In other words, it was clear everybody thought the idea of a model fly-fishing regulation was just great so long as it didn't interfere with the way *they* fished. Unfortunately, they fished in so many different ways there was nothing left for the committee to regulate.

It was obvious there was little or no chance of reaching agreement, so the federation suspended the committee's work to let things cool off until the time might be ripe to try again. A couple of decades have passed and the time has never ripened.

Looking back on it now, I suppose we were naive to think that anglers ever could or would agree on such a regulation or definition. This is a broad land, and local fishing conditions and traditions vary widely—probably too widely ever to impose a standard definition or set of rules that could apply fairly in all circumstances. Besides, those states that already have fly-fishing regulations generally have done a good job of defining the sport to fit local needs and conditions, and it doesn't seem unreasonable to expect that when anglers go fishing in another state they should first obtain a copy of the local regulations and read it.

So perhaps we never needed a model regulation or definition of fly fishing in the first place. On the other hand, I think there are some good reasons why we do.

Those reasons have to do with the unique quality of fly fishing as a sport that considers the means more important than the end, one that places a greater value on skill than on results. Or, to put it another way, the essence of fly fishing is that *how* we catch fish matters as much or more as *whether* we catch them.

Think about that for a moment. If bagging fish were our only objective, we would be better off using dynamite, spears or nets. Instead, by choosing to be fly fishers, we have voluntarily placed certain limits on ourselves and accepted a challenge to develop the skills necessary to overcome those limits. The true test of a fly fisher is how well he or she learns and practices these skills. It is the integrity of that concept that needs to be protected by definition.

Why should we be concerned about this? One reason is that fly fishing has experienced explosive growth in popularity and commercial attention in recent years. Many newcomers have adapted quickly to the traditions and values of the sport, but others have not. Some, in fact, have gotten it all wrong; they see fly fishing as only another way of catching fish, equating success with the number of dead trout in their creel. Others seek only to profit from the sport by marketing questionable shortcuts to skills that usually take years of practice to acquire, or by selling tackle or other gadgets designed to bypass the need for such skills altogether. Still others view the sport as a means to acquire a reputation by taking part in misguided fishing competitions or trying to capture meaningless records.

Of course we have always had some of this sort of thing, but I think there is rather more of it now than ever before. Contemporary books, articles, films and advertisements offer plenty of evidence that a willing market exists for items that promise convenience or expediency to fly fishers. While there's nothing inherently wrong with that, the integrity of the sport inevitably suffers whenever the price of these items requires surrendering traditional values and ethics.

That's why I believe it's time we had a good definition of what fly fishing is—and, just as important, what it is not.

Such a definition need not be rigid or confining, as Halford's was; indeed, it should be broad and flexible enough to encourage the freedom of expression and experimentation that is essential for the future progress of the sport. In fact, it should be nothing more than a general endorsement of the principle that in fly fishing the means is always more important than the end, and that attainment of skill is the highest aim.

Such a definition would still leave room for ethical differences on questions such as those concerning the legitimacy of the angling methods described at the beginning of this essay. But if fly fishers could agree on a basic definition of their sport, then at least their differences would be rooted in common ground, and there would be much more to unite them than to divide them.

Yet fly fishers are such a disparate and stubborn lot that it's probably wishful and idealistic thinking to expect they could ever agree on much of anything. Nevertheless, despite the odds, the quest for a definition strikes me as an effort still worth making, no matter how long it may take.

And if, somehow, we ever do agree on one, we will have taken a giant step toward protecting the integrity of our sport as one truly founded on the notion that what's really important is not whether you win or lose; what really matters is how you play the game.

AUTHOR'S NOTES

Many of the essays in this book were published previously. Where appropriate, they have been revised, edited or otherwise adapted for use in this book. They are listed here in order of their appearance in the preceding pages.

"A CALM, QUIET, INNOCENT RECREATION"
 "By the Book" was originally published in *Sports Illustrated*, May 10, 1982.
 "Shop Scents" was first published in shorter form in *Sports Illustrated*, April 8, 1985.
 "The Fine Art of Flyfinagling" was originally published in *The Flyfisher*, No. 5, summer 1969. It is, of course, mostly fictional, including the "obscure, seldom published" version of *The Treatyse on Fysshynge with an Angle*. But there really *is* an enduring legend that Daniel Webster caught a monster trout in Long Island's Carmans River.
 "Junkyard Rivers" was originally published in *Sports Illustrated*, March 16, 1981.
 "Dressing for Success" was originally published in *FlyFishing*, November–December 1993.
 "Bear with Me" is published here for the first time.
 "The Intrepid Insect Trapper" was originally published in *Fly Fisherman*, Vol. 33, No. 3, March 2002.

"Elko Interlude" was originally published in *Western FlyFishing,* July–October 1995.

"Playing the Numbers" was originally published in *FlyFishing,* April 1995.

You Should Have Been Here Yesterday

"The Good Old Days" is based on a presentation to the Washington Fly Fishing Club, Seattle, in February 2001. James G. Swan's oft-published diary, *The Northwest Coast,* is now in the public domain, as is the report of the Northern Pacific Railroad Survey. I am indebted to the late angling historian Austin Hogan for the transcript of William Merry's articles in *American Angler.* The Lambuth diary was given me by his widow, Olive Lambuth, and the two Bradner manuscripts were given me by Bradner himself before his death. The Lambuth and Bradner documents are now in the archives of the Washington Fly Fishing Club.

"Fishing with Bill Nation" is adapted from a presentation to the annual general meeting of the British Columbia Federation of Fly Fishers in Kamloops, BC, in May 2000, later published in *Fly Lines,* the BCFFF quarterly publication, Vol. 4, No. 1, summer–fall 2003. I am grateful to BC angling historian Arthur Lingren for sharing copies of some of Nation's correspondence.

"Remembering Ralph Wahl" first appeared in shorter form in *The Osprey,* published by the Steelhead Committee of the Federation of Fly Fishers, Issue No. 46, September 2003. Wahl's collection of fishing photos is now in the archives of the Center for Pacific Northwest Studies at Western Washington University, Bellingham.

Causes and Controversies

"Sensitivity Training" was originally published in *FlyFishing,* November–December 1994.

"Wives and Lovers" has been revised from a presentation to the Evergreen Fly Fishing Club in Everett, Washington, December 1972.

"Fish Culture" was originally published in *FlyFishing*, July–October 1996.

"Boob Tubes" was first published in shorter form as "Too Much of a Good Thing" in *Fly Fisherman*, Vol. 23, No. 2, February 1992.

"The *Salmo* Society" was originally published in *Western Fly-Fishing*, January–February 1996.

MEMORIES ARE MADE OF FISH

"Opening Daze" was originally published in *Western FlyFishing*, March–April 1997.

"The Beaver-Pond Brotherhood" was originally published in *Fly Fisherman*, Vol. 31, No. 4, May 2000.

"Rescue Mission" was originally published in *Western FlyFishing*, June 1996.

"How Now Brown Trout" is published here for the first time.

"Early and Late" was originally published in *Western FlyFishing*, June 1997.

"Shad Occasion" was originally published in slightly different form in *Fly Fisherman*, Vol. 34, No. 5, July 2003.

"Monday Night Salmon" was originally published in shorter form in *Sports Illustrated*, February 15, 1982. It has been expanded and updated to reflect Dr. Al Adams' latest efforts to preserve and enhance salmon.

"February" was originally published in *Western FlyFishing*, January–February 1997.

"Yesterday's Magic" was originally published in *FlyFishing*, July–October 1994.

THE STATE OF THE ART

"Take Me to Your Leader" was originally published in *Western FlyFishing*, November–December 1996.

"The Arcane Art" was originally published in *FlyFishing*, January–February, 1994.

"Coping with Technology" was originally published in *FlyFishing*, June 1994.

"'Old Yeller'" was originally published in *Fly Fisherman*, Vol. 37, No. 3, March 2006.

"The Compleat Fly Tyer" was originally published under the title "Fly Tying Is an Art" in *The Flyfisher*, Vol. III, No. 2, 1970. John W. and his backyard menagerie are fictional, but I have known some real-life fly tyers whose pursuit of the art was scarcely less fanatical.

"Silver Bullets and Exploding Floatants" is published here for the first time.

"The Sound of Silence" was originally published in *Fly Fisherman*, Vol. 35, No. 5, July 2004.

"A Matter of Definition" was originally published in *Fly Fisherman*, Vol. 17, No. 2, December 1985.